CONTESTED PERCEPTIONS

Interactions and Relations
between China, Korea, and Japan
since the Seventeenth Century

OKAMOTO Takashi

Japan Publishing Industry Foundation for Culture

Publisher's Note
This book follows the Hepburn system of romanization for Japanese, the McCune-Reischauer system for Korean, and the Pinyin system for the names of some places and works in Chinese. Japanese, Chinese, and Korean names are written in their conventional order of family name followed by given name. Except for place names on maps, long vowels in names and book titles are indicated by macrons.

Disclaimer: Every effort has been taken to trace copyright holders for the photographs in this publication. The publisher welcomes correspondence from those who were unable to be contacted.

Contested Perceptions: Interactions and Relations between China, Korea, and Japan since the Seventeenth Century
Okamoto Takashi. Translated by the Japan Institute of International Affairs (JIIA).

Published by
Japan Publishing Industry Foundation for Culture (JPIC)
2-2-30 Kanda-Jinbocho, Chiyoda-ku, Tokyo 101-0051, Japan

First English edition: March 2022

© 2008 Okamoto Takashi
English translation © 2022 The Japan Institute of International Affairs (JIIA)
All rights reserved

Originally published in Japanese under the title *Sekai no naka no Nis-Shin-Kan kankeishi: Kōrin to zokkoku, jishu to dokuritsu* by Kodansha Ltd. in 2008.
English publishing rights arranged with Kodansha Ltd., Tokyo.

This publication is the result of a collaborative effort between the Japan Institute of International Affairs (JIIA) and Japan Publishing Industry Foundation for Culture (JPIC).

Book design: alema Co., Ltd.

Printed in Japan
ISBN 978-4-86658-231-3
https://www.jpic.or.jp/

Table of Contents

Independent Autonomy

Preface

More than a decade has passed since this book was published in Japanese. My goal in writing it was to communicate my latest findings on the foreign relations of nineteenth-century China. I strove to present my ideas in a way that would be easily understood yet maintain a rigorous academic tone. At the time I had not envisioned a non-Japanese audience. That a text of mine would be available to English readers around the world comes as an unexpected joy.

Today, we inhabit a world in which the "sovereign state," a notion of Western European origin, has become ubiquitous. The grip this paradigm holds over us in the present day often makes it difficult for us to realize that other modes of interaction between polities existed in the "pre-modern" world. East Asia is a case in point. Just one hundred years ago, up until the advent of the twentieth century, the region operated according to a set of principles that is wholly unrecognizable from the sovereign state system of today.

As a consequence of China's rapid transformation into a global power, this historical East Asian paradigm has recently drawn increased levels of attention. This is because the legacy of this pre-existing order continues to color and influence many of the actions modern China engages in today.

Historically speaking, the Korean Peninsula played a key role in this order. Since ancient times, the region has had a significant impact on mainland China and the Japanese archipelago. This situation persists today, with Korea continuing to exert a decisive influence upon

East Asian politics. There is no getting around it: analyzing the situation in East Asia today requires us to contemplate the historical relations of China, Korea, and Japan. Indeed, the present power balance between these states emerged no later than in the sixteenth century. Accordingly, certain aspects of the current state of affairs cannot be properly understood unless viewed through the lens of that era.

Japanese warlord Toyotomi Hideyoshi's (1537–1598) military expeditions into Korea, and the rise to power of early modern Japan that enabled them, catalyzed the emergence of this power balance. Given the critical geopolitical position of the Korean Peninsula, for the land-based state and maritime state that sat at either side, its capture by the other could spell life or death. As such, for the next two hundred years, order and peace were ensured by a delicate balancing of relationships, with Korea as fulcrum.

However, in the nineteenth century, the Western powers advanced into East Asia, and Japan commenced a program of modernization that eventually aspired to the national ideal of "enriching the country and strengthening the military." The delicate balance among China, Korea, and Japan fell apart, upsetting the existing order and creating a configuration that would persist into the modern era. This development came from the question of whether Korea should be treated as a "tributary" or recognized as "autonomous," and would ultimately lead to the First Sino-Japanese War (1894–1895).

As a consequence, at the dawn of the twentieth century, the Korean kingdom became the Korean Empire, achieving "independent sovereignty" from Qing China. However, the situation in East Asia remained unstable, which allowed Japan to annex the Korean Empire in 1910.

This historical process, which I explore in this book, is still playing out today. The Korean Peninsula remains divided, and this political problem continues to sow the seeds of regional instability. The increased prominence of China on the world stage has also brought further great change both to the international situation and to the Korean Peninsula. These factors make East Asia's future all the more uncertain. Building a stable order there is therefore a task of historic import that demands all the wisdom at our disposal.

Of course, a lone historian has neither the credentials nor the capability to analyze present affairs or to comment on how the future may play out. What I can say is that the present is a product of the past and a springboard for the future. More than anything else, I believe that studying the facts of history engenders an accurate comprehension of the present and the creation of a better tomorrow. Nothing would please me more than for my book to help realize that end.

The publication of this English-language edition owes much to many individuals. Particular thanks go to the following people: to Trans-Asia, Inc., for their considered translation; to Word House, Ltd., for their editorial finesse and careful handling of the text; to Thomas P. Barrett, for his specialist expertise and invaluable writing suggestions; to Shikata Chihiro, a researcher of public diplomacy at the Japan Institute of International Affairs (JIIA); and to Nakaizumi Kiyoshi and Oka Mariyo, of the Japan Publishing Industry Foundation for Culture (JPIC).

Okamoto Takashi
November 2021

Map of Qing China, Korea, Japan, and Russia in the Nineteenth Century

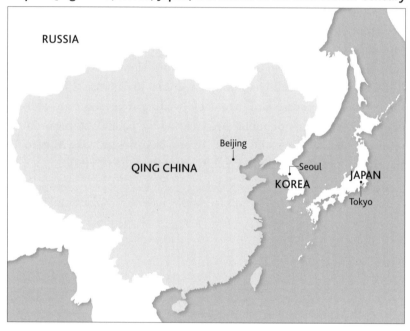

Introduction

The Death of a Prime Minister

The Blue House (Ch'ŏngwadae) is the office of the South Korean president. To its south lies Kyŏngbok Palace, which may be considered the Korean Chosŏn (Joseon) dynasty's answer to the Forbidden City in Beijing. It is a major tourist attraction. Kwanghwa Gate, the main gate of the palace, burned down during the Korean War but was reconstructed years later, during President Pak Chŏnghŭi's term of office (1963–1979). In 2010, the reconstruction was relocated to the site where the original once stood.

On February 11, 1896, Prime Minister Kim Hongjip was killed by a mob outside Kwanghwa Gate. He was fifty-five years old.

The death of a country's prime minister is a serious incident, and Kim Hongjip's killing is referenced in all Korean history texts. Even so, I have never seen it treated as a standalone topic. It is instead related as an anecdote of the period.

When we unravel the threads of history, we find that countless prime ministers have been murdered across all times and places. The only reason that the Japanese are apt to think of it as strange is perhaps because such incidents have been rare in Japan. Even so, there are the cases of Hara Takashi and Inukai Tsuyoshi, two twentieth-century prime ministers who were assassinated. If we include cabinet ministers and other former prime ministers, then such incidents seem less uncommon than the Japanese have been prone to suppose. This is all the more true of the Chosŏn dynasty, in which political strife had been

Kwanghwa Gate
Photo from Kyodo News

a constant for generations and the political situation mired in instability. As such, we might make allowances for those who do not pay much attention to assassination and who consider it to be a common historical event.

However, I have never heard of a sequence of events as bizarre as this: a prime minister, perfectly cognizant of his imminent assassination, openly marches toward an angry mob while proclaiming, "It is the will of Heaven," and then proceeds to be murdered. While I am not confident enough to rule out that something like this never happened before at any other point in history, I doubt there are many examples. I believe it is precisely this perverse state of affairs that can provide us with some sense of the situation Korea faced at this historical juncture.

Kim Hongjip's assassination happened immediately after the First Sino-Japanese War. This was a period in which, with Japanese support, Kim made repeated attempts at forming a cabinet and was deeply engaged in a process of political reform. However, he incurred considerable opposition for making it his policy to separate the king and queen from the government and to exclude them from political participation. Then, in October 1895, when Japan brought about the murder of Queen Min at Kyŏngbok Palace, Kim Hongjip, in accordance with Japanese wishes, sought to settle the issue without clearly assigning blame to any party. This act cost him all support from King Kojong.

Moreover, the conservative landed elites, who valued their traditional customs, opposed one of Kim's reforms, which prohibited the growing or wearing of topknots. As the new year dawned, these same elites, filled with rage at the barbaric murder of the queen, mobilized the Korean people, whose own anti-Japanese sentiment had grown stronger, and intensified their opposition to the Kim Hongjip administration.

Amid this disquieting atmosphere, King Kojong, who had feared for his life since the killing of Queen Min, joined forces with pro-Russian officials who had been ousted from the regime. They soon fled Kyŏngbok Palace to seek refuge in the Russian legation, where they formed a new government. As part of this move, they ruled that Kim Hongjip and other key persons in the old regime were criminals, and ordered their arrest.

The resulting coup d'état succeeded in bringing down the regime. It was likely that it was Kim Hongjip's despair over his complete loss of support from both officialdom and the public that led to such calm acceptance of his fate.

The Life and Times of Kim Hongjip

Kim Hongjip's violent death could be reasonably understood as an inevitable consequence of his support for Japanese aggression against Korea. Even so, the Korean political situation at that time was far too complex for us to consider this the sole explanation for all that transpired.

Kim Hongjip's family clan seat was in Kyŏngju, and he used the pen names Towŏn and Ijŏnghakchae. In 1868, at age twenty-seven, he passed the civil service examination and joined the ranks of Korean officialdom. Oddly enough, this was also the year that Korea came

Korean prime minister Kim Hongjip (1842–1896)

Reprinted from *Kim Hongjip yugo* [Posthumous Manuscripts of Kim Hongjip] (Seoul: Korea University Press, 1976).

into conflict with the newly constituted Meiji Japanese state over the Japanese use of the Chinese title of "emperor" in relation to their own head of state in their diplomatic documents. In addition, the Korean purge of Catholics, the ensuing punitive French expedition to Korea, and the *General Sherman* incident had all taken place just two years prior. Kim Hongjip's political debut in autumn of 1868 thus constituted a watershed moment in Korean history. Indeed, under outside pressure, Korea had been compelled to court the Western world and to brave the storm of nineteenth-century international politics.

Thereafter, having risen steadily in rank, Kim reached the first turning point of his career: his involvement in negotiations with Japan, with whom Korea had signed the Treaty of Kanghwa in 1876.

Although the treaty had been signed by both parties, there were disagreements about the particulars of its implementation, including tariffs and items of trade. The parties accordingly conducted additional negotiations. In 1880, Kim went to Japan to represent Korea in these negotiations as the second friendship envoy (J. *shūshinshi*, K. *susinsa*) of the Chosŏn mission to Meiji Japan. Given Kim's role in such important events, it would be fair to say that it was he who ushered in the 1880s, which saw the start of an increasingly unstable situation in East Asia.

Around the same time, Qing China had opened a diplomatic mission in Japan, and appointed He Ruzhang as its first minister in residence. Kim Hongjip called on He Ruzhang at the Chinese legation in Shiba, Tokyo. There, he received instruction not only about his ongoing negotiations with Japan but also about the foreign policy Korea should adopt going forward. He returned with the pamphlet *Chaoxian celüe* (Strategy for Korea, 1880), written by Huang Zunxian, one of He Ruzhang's subordinates. This pamphlet, which recommended that Korea conclude a treaty with the United States and strengthen its relations with Qing China, is renowned for serving as the impetus for Korea's conclusion of treaties with the Western powers.

It was these experiences that led to Kim Hongjip's coming to be regarded as an expert in foreign negotiations. He was subsequently called on to play an important role whenever diplomatic negotiations were conducted. In 1881, he was appointed accounting official of the Office for the Management of State Affairs. In 1882, he was made second minister of the Board of Personnel and of the Board of Works, as well as senior official of the Deliberative Council. It was at this time that he was also appointed as treaty negotiation vice-official for the treaties with the United States, Britain, and Germany, becoming the de facto Korean representative plenipotentiary. In this capacity, he saw the treaties successfully signed, working closely with Ma Jianzhong, who had been dispatched from Qing China to oversee the dynasty's Korea policy.

Subsequently, in response to the Imo Incident of summer 1882, Kim shuttled busily between Japan and Qing China. With guidance from Ma Jianzhong, he led the difficult negotiations with Japan. He not only concluded the Chemulp'o Treaty but was dispatched to Beijing immediately afterward to participate in devising remedial measures as well. During this time, Kim also earned the confidence of Ma Jianzhong, with Ma going so far as to describe him as "wise and discerning about current affairs" and "likely the greatest person in Korea."

A Pro-Chinese or Pro-Japanese Diplomat?

The foregoing suggests that Kim Hongjip initially stood closer to Qing China than to Japan, which was precisely the case.

He refused to participate in the Kapsin Coup—an attempted coup d'état carried out at the end of 1884 by Kim Okkyun and his peers to seize political power with the help of Japanese influence. Moreover, in the settlement negotiations of the following year, he was unyielding. He thoroughly tormented his counterpart, the Japanese plenipotentiary and minister for foreign affairs Inoue Kaoru.

Tracing Kim Hongjip's career in this way shows he was by no means a "pro-Japanese" diplomat who supported Japanese aggression against Korea. Rather, he cooperated with Qing China, opposed Japan, and sought to suppress the pro-Japanese domestic Korean faction. His efforts did not go unnoticed. Indeed, he, his discernment, and his talents came to be highly esteemed by the Chinese side. He was unequivocally pro-Chinese.

In the second half of the 1880s, however, his pro-Chinese stance caused him to be forced into a sinecure. This was because the Korean court came to favor a policy of keeping Qing China at more of a distance than Japan. This was the same person branded as "pro-Japanese" and murdered some ten years later. What were the circumstances that had led to this shift in allegiances?

Since Kim Hongjip had become the head of the Korean cabinet by gaining the support of Japan after the defeat of Qing China in the First Sino-Japanese War, we might say that Kim Hongjip defected, to use common parlance. Although that may be correct in itself, what made him do so? Moreover, why did he have no choice but to die?

Furthermore, following Kim's violent death, a strange situation came about in which the Korean court and government were housed in a foreign legation. What would be the outcome of these events?

The scope of such questions goes beyond the person of Kim Hongjip. It even goes beyond the country of Korea itself. We should look for answers instead in the movements of East Asian history.

CHAPTER ONE

Tributary Relations

1. The Foreign Relations of the Chosŏn Dynasty

Chinese Civilization and Korea

The Chosŏn dynasty was founded by T'aejo Yi Sŏnggye in 1392 after the overthrow of the Koryŏ Wang dynasty. Since its establishment, the dynasty had maintained intimate ties with the Chinese Ming dynasty. One example of this intimacy came with the choice of its name. Indeed, the name "Chosŏn," of ancient and honorable origin, was not itself chosen by the Koreans. Rather, it was bestowed upon the dynasty by the Ming.

One further example of this intimacy was the fact that the Chosŏn dynasty constituted the polity most loyal to the worldview and world order envisioned by the Ming. Drawing upon Confucianism and neo-Confucianism in particular, this worldview posited the Ming as sitting at the center of a world in which its relations with neighboring countries were predicated upon an ordered system of rites that took, as its underlying basis, the distinction between "civility" and "barbarity," and the "duty to one's sovereign." This world order goes by many names in academia, such as the "tributary system," the "tribute trade system," and "Chinese World Order." All of them make sense to some degree, making it difficult to stick with just one. Hereinafter, so as to be faithful to the terminology of the historical sources and to avoid unnecessary confusion and misunderstanding, I will refer to the relationship between Ming China and the countries which subscribed to its worldview as a *zongfan* relationship (this terminology will be further elaborated upon hereinafter).

According to this worldview, the Ming emperors were mandated by "Heaven" to rule the world. They were thus the "Sons of Heaven" reigning over Chinese civilization, which was itself taken to be the center of the world. Neighboring countries surrounding China were accordingly meant to respect that heavenly mandate, thereby serving and swearing allegiance to the Ming emperors. As proof of their allegiance, the leaders of these neighboring countries would bring products from their countries to the Son of Heaven as tribute. Having received these gifts, the Ming emperors responded not only by bestowing extensive gifts of their own but also by showing their approval of the neighboring countries' rulers.

These actions on the part of the neighboring countries are called "tribute," whereas those performed by the Ming are known as "investiture." This is why this relationship is commonly referred to as a "tributary system" or, as it is sometimes referred to in Japan, an "investiture framework."

Fourteenth-century Japan was no exception, since the rulers of Japan paid tribute and received investiture. Specifically, the shogun Ashikaga Yoshimitsu was invested as "King of Japan" by the Ming emperor and was allowed to conduct licensed trade with the Ming. However, given the independence of the Japanese "king," such a configuration makes it clear that ideological deference to Ming China did not necessarily mean that the dynasty exercised any effective rule or influence over the domestic affairs of neighboring countries.

At the same time, for Japan, the articulation of ideological deference to the Ming and the payment of tribute did not necessarily equate to wholesale subscription to the Ming worldview. Rather, there were more pragmatic reasons underlying its choice to engage in such performances: namely, trade with the dynasty. However, such a situation did not apply only to Japan. These performances were essential for the vast majority of neighboring countries who wanted to conduct trade with Ming China.

The sole exception in this regard was Korea. While Japan, together with China's other neighboring countries, was largely indifferent to, ignorant of, and uninterested in this neo-Confucian order, the Chosŏn dynasty embraced neo-Confucianism as a national ideology and, as a corollary, subscribed wholesale to the Ming worldview.

By accepting the world order envisioned by the Ming, the Chosŏn dynasty revered the Ming as its superior state (C. *zong*), and contented itself with its status as a tributary (C. *fan* or *fanshu*). This is why scholars use the term *zongfan*, although in more common parlance, we might refer to this relationship as one based on flunkeyism. In the Korean context, however, the *zongfan* relationship with the Ming was also known as a *sadae* relationship, or a relationship of "serving-the-great." "*Sa*" means to "to serve," while "*dae*" refers to a "great country" or *taeguk*. One other synonym of *taeguk* used by Korea was *sangguk*, or superior country. During the Ming era, both of these terms referred to none other than Ming China itself. Following the strictures of neo-Confucianism, Korea treated the Ming as a lord in accordance with the ritual of propriety found between sovereign and minister, or between father and son. In this book, I will use the term "serving-the-great" when describing Korea's *zongfan* relationship with China from the Korean perspective.

Serving-the-Great and *Kyorin* (Neighborly Relations)

This *zongfan* relationship between Korea and the Ming constituted the central component of Korea's foreign relations. However, Ming China was not the only polity with whom it maintained relations, nor was this *zongfan* relationship the only means through which Korea interacted with the outside world. After all, to Korea's south was the Japanese archipelago and the Okinawan islands, and to its north, the region beyond the Yalu River (Amnok River) that today constitutes the Chinese provinces of Liaoning and Jilin.

Historical maps indicate that by the time the Ming dynasty had reached its peak during the reign of the Yongle emperor (r. 1402–1424), the dynasty had come to control almost all of the lands bordering on Korea. However, as the dynasty weakened, its influence in the northeast was reduced to just the Liaodong Peninsula. This resulted in the mouth of the Yalu River becoming the only point of contact between Ming China and Korea.

Korea's geographical position necessitated interactions with non-Ming polities. Sandwiched in-between itself and Ming China was a sparsely populated forest belt inhabited by the Tungusic Jurchen people (present-day Manchuria). What is more, to its south were Japan and the Ryukyu Kingdom (present-day Okinawa).

As I will explain below, Korea took a unique stance toward its Jurchen, Japanese, and Ryukyuan neighbors. It referred to these relationships using the term "*kyorin*," which literally translates to "neighborly relations." The adjective "neighborly" is, however, somewhat misleading. Indeed, the nuances and sentiments encapsulated by the concept of *kyorin* were something else again.

In order to understand the underlying connotations of the "neighborly relations" concept, it is important to bear in mind that Chosŏn Korea revered neo-Confucianism as much as or perhaps even more than the Ming. Accordingly, the Koreans were very particular about the neo-Confucian distinction between civility and barbarity. They even viewed themselves as barbarians when compared to the Ming, whom they saw as the genuine inheritors of Chinese civilization.

Despite such deprecatory self-perception, Korea's profound admiration for Chinese civilization instilled in its elite a desire to achieve perfect emulation of its protocols, rituals, and values. Indeed, Korea tasked itself with becoming a perfect facsimile of Chinese civilization, giving itself names such as "Decorous Country in the East," "Eastern China," and "Little China." From such a vantage point, the Japanese, Ryukyuans, and Jurchen were nothing more than barbarians or savages.

Despite its efforts to achieve perfect mimesis of Chinese civilization, its diminutive status vis-à-vis Ming China meant that it was not possible for Korea to initiate *zongfan* relationships with its neighbors. This was a privilege reserved for the Ming and the Ming alone. From the perspective of the Ming, all of Korea's neighbors were tributary states who subscribed to Ming primacy. As such, Korea had no choice but to treat its non-Ming neighbors on ostensibly equal terms, applying a uniform principle of equality. The connotation of the term "equality" in this context was that all of Korea's neighbors were to be treated as though on an equal footing with Korea, even if they were adversaries.

However, relations between Korea and its non-Ming neighbors were only ever *ostensibly* based on a premise of equality. At heart, Korea disdained the Japanese, Ryukyuans, and Jurchen, viewing them as lowly barbarians and inhuman beasts. This is why Korea's relations with its non-Ming neighbors never took place according to a standardized format of protocol like that of tribute and investiture that characterized the Ming's *zongfan* relationships.

Korea's foreign relations were thus predicated on two fundamental principles: "serving-the-great" and "neighborly relations." However, the precise means through which these principles were enacted varied according to the party involved. The principle of serving-the-great applied only to Korea's relationship with the Ming. Meanwhile, although the principle of neighborly relations was employed universally for its non-Ming relationships, these "neighborly" relationships were each enacted according to their own unique set of bilateral circumstances, and were unaffected by any other relationship which operated according to this principle. For instance, Korea's neighborly ties with Japan took a form specific to relations with Japan and did not apply to any other "neighborly" relationship. The precise specificities of each of Korea's relationships with its neighbors were thus extremely difficult to comprehend unless one was a direct participant.

Given such circumstances, understanding the niceties of the Ming-Chosŏn *zongfan* relationship would have been no easy task for Japan to achieve. Even today, many aspects of this historical relationship continue to perplex. The same can likely be said of China in trying to understand the relationship between Korea and Japan.

It was only the Chosŏn dynasty who could impart meaning to these relationships and the principles that undergirded them. Furthermore, it was through this process of ascribing meaning, and the selection of specific principles for specific bilateral relationships, that Chosŏn fostered its own unique perspective on the world and its underlying patterns of order. Any Japanese or Chinese perspective on one of Chosŏn's individual bilateral relationships would inevitably constitute a jaundiced refraction of how Chosŏn *itself* understood these relationships. Unlike in the modern world, in which international law serves as a guiding set of principles for relations between states, there existed no shared normative paradigm that regulated interactions between East Asian countries in the early modern world.

However, Chosŏn's decidedly singular approach to foreign relations would by no means last forever. The coming of the Age of Discovery in the sixteenth century would fundamentally transform how Chosŏn interacted with the outside world.

2. The Japanese Disturbances

The Rise of Japan in World and East Asian History

The islands of the Japanese archipelago are scattered along the far eastern edge of the Eurasian continent. Beyond the islands to the east lies nothing but a vast expanse of open sea. Given this position, the islands constitute a world unto itself for which the name "the Far East" is truly appropriate.

The ancient Chinese view of Japan was that of a somewhat unruly land in the eastern sea, divided into many provinces. Prince Shōtoku is credited with having established the first centralized government in Japan. This happened at the start of the seventh century, around the time of the Sui and Tang dynasties in China. With this achievement, the prince, calling himself "the sovereign of the Land of the Rising Sun," was at last able to represent the whole of Japan and dispatch envoys on Japan's behalf. However, despite such developments, the world remained largely insouciant to these sweeping changes.

Indeed, it would be fair to say that Japan did not make much of an impression on the world until the latter part of the thirteenth century, during the Mongol invasions. These were a series of failed attempts at conquest of the archipelago, and came at a time when a large part of the world was under Mongol rule or influence. The only regions on the Eurasian continent to escape Mongol conquest were Europe at the western end and Japan at the eastern end.

The failure of the Mongols to successfully conquer Japan and Europe may simply have been a result of geography and how far the

Mongol Empire could project its military might. However, I would like to suggest that there were far more profound reasons underlying the failure of these invasions. The eighteenth and nineteenth centuries demonstrated that it was only the regions which sat at the eastern and western edges of the Eurasian continent that possessed social structures conducive to capitalist development. This fact alone indicates that Japan and Europe differed significantly from most of Eurasia.

At any rate, after the Mongol invasions of the thirteenth century, Japan had no choice but to begin a much more substantial engagement with the Chinese mainland and the Korean Peninsula than before. Japan's success in staving off Mongol incursions had also given it a much more prominent position in the Chinese and Korean imaginations: it could pose a threat. It is widely known that the founder of the Ming dynasty counted Japan as one of the "countries that we should not attempt to conquer" and even feared that Japan might collude with rebellious ministers. Likewise, Japanese pirates were heavily implicated in the process that led to the founding of the Chosŏn dynasty as well.

Seen from China and Korea, Japan was, therefore, an uncomfortable presence. Such sentiment could be noted in the term used in Chinese to refer to the Japanese pirates that ravaged the seas: *wokou* (J. *wakō*). The term carried connotations of a violent threat from across the sea.

It therefore did not come as a surprise to China and Korea to learn, both through firsthand experiences of and research on Japanese society, that the country was dominated by military men and was utterly devoid of the so-called "sagely way" that characterized the cultures of Confucian countries. This perspective was especially true for China and Korea's Confucian literati for whom not war, but the reading, writing, and keeping of records was the defining characteristic of bureaucratic life.

For the Chinese and the Koreans, the Japanese were beyond the pale of any of their systems of Confucian ideology or ethics. Indeed, for them, the Japanese were an unpredictable presence who did not operate according to any prescribed body of conduct, and must have been something truly unpleasant and incomprehensible. Even today, the general feeling of many Chinese, South Koreans, and North Koreans toward Japan may well be close to this sentiment of the past.

Japanese historian and sinologist Naitō Konan famously said that to know Japan, one does not need to know anything prior to the Ōnin War (a civil conflict from 1467 to 1477), just that which followed. While Naitō himself was specifically referring to Japanese history, in many ways these words of his are all the more apt in the context of world history. The reason for this is because this postbellum period constituted a turning point from which Japan came to exert a more profound influence upon Asia and, by extension, upon world history.

This was the sixteenth-century Age of Discovery, when the New World was discovered and the power of the West made its way eastward. It coincided with a sudden increase in the production of silver, which started circulating around the world. The increased silver production would further vitalize Chinese society, which had, by this point, undergone significant structural changes and was starting to develop economically. The Japanese archipelago, with its rich deposits of precious metals, also suddenly emerged as a new and important trading partner thanks to the development of its mines and the resulting production of gold and silver. The result was rapidly amplified Japanese power.

This amplification of Japanese power brought several key developments. First came the Sengoku (Warring States) period (1467–1568, of which the aforementioned Ōnin War is generally considered the earliest phase), in which rival Japanese warlords vied for supremacy. The conflict culminated in the unification of Japan in the Azuchi-Momoyama period (1568–1603). The consequent convergence from local conflicts to national consolidation resulted in a magnification of domestic wealth and military might. In turn, this same domestic wealth and military might came to exert an influence externally in the seas around China. This was the era of the so-called late-period *wokou*, or Japanese pirates.

As the sixteenth century drew to a close, although Japanese piracy had begun to wane, on an external front, Japan remained far from satiated. This mentality culminated in the Korean expeditions of Toyotomi

Hideyoshi, the warlord who had initiated the aforementioned quest to reunify Japan under a central authority.

The Korean Expeditions

In Toyotomi's own words, these foreign campaigns were launched with the motive of leading the way "into China." That said, it is unclear what their true goal was. It is easy to dismiss them as self-righteous acts and delusions of grandeur far removed from the actual circumstances of East Asia. It is also obvious that such campaigns would be unsuccessful. Even so, the impact of the launch and failure of these campaigns was enormous.

The campaigns served as the impetus for an irrevocable break within the Toyotomi regime between the military exploit faction that advocated war, and the faction of government officials that advocated peace. With the death of Toyotomi, the reins of government passed to Tokugawa Ieyasu. Tokugawa then brought about the Edo *bakufu* (the government of the Tokugawa shogunate) after his victory in the Battle of Sekigahara (1600).

But the campaigns' impact went far beyond Japanese domestic politics. Nearly all of Korea's territory was violated, and the damage is said to have defied description. These military campaigns of 1592 and 1597, corresponding to the Japanese eras of Bunroku (1592–96) and Keichō (1596–1615), are known in Korea as the "Japanese Disturbance of Imjin" and the "Japanese Disturbance of Chŏngyu," respectively. The prevailing fear of Japan as a violent threat had indeed become a reality. There are, however, matters to be discussed with regard to the Korean side as well.

In the first place, the Chosŏn dynasty was a centralized bureaucratic state that systematically favored men of letters. The dynasty, across all levels of social strata, disparaged and looked down upon men of military backgrounds in accordance with the premises of Confucianism and neo-Confucianism. The result of this thinking was that its military power was relatively unimpressive.

The dynasty had nonetheless long remained safe from external threats. That was because the aforementioned arrangements of "serving-the-great" and "neighborly relations" had functioned reasonably well, meaning that diplomacy had worked as it should. Conversely, a mistake in the conduct of diplomacy would have entailed considerable risk of an immediate foreign threat, where a neighboring country with superior military power was concerned.

It was for these reasons that in the latter half of the fifteenth century, Sin Sukchu, who guided Korea's foreign policy in his capacity as minister of the Board of Rites and chief state councillor, defined his role as maintaining the dynasty's relationships with China and neighboring countries according to the principles of "serving-the-great" and "neighborly relations" above all else. In achieving this goal, his greatest concern was Japan.

Sin first visited the country as an envoy in 1443 at the age of twenty-seven. In his later years, he authored an important book, published in 1471, titled *Haedong chegukki* (Records of Countries across the Sea to the East), which offers us an insight into his research on Japan and Japanese-Korean relations at the time. The following is a famous excerpt:

> Their nature is intrepid, their swordsmanship skillful, and their boatmanship experienced. We gaze at each other from either side of the sea. If we find a means to pacify them, they will come to participate in the exchange of envoys. However, if we lose that means, they will resort to reckless piracy.*

If, in this way, the Koreans viewed Japan as a threat, then they should have been alert to the transformation Japan was undergoing at the end of the Sengoku period and have made the appropriate preparations. Yet it would seem that the concerns of Sin Sukchu did not find consensus in the Korean government.

---

*All translations from Korean and Chinese sources have been translated from the Japanese text that features in the original 2008 edition of this book.

Following Sin Sukchu's death in the latter half of the fifteenth century, the Chosŏn dynasty ceased to dispatch Korean envoys to Japan. This decision inevitably resulted in Korea becoming less attuned to the Japanese situation. It was for this reason that, by the end of the sixteenth century, the Koreans, in fruitless adherence to moral obligations, averted their gaze from the actual circumstances in Japan at the time. They misinterpreted the reality of the transition from the Sengoku period to the Toyotomi regime. Even with the start of Toyotomi's Korean expeditions, the Koreans only attempted to conduct negotiations via, on the one hand, the Sō (a clan which governed the Japanese-controlled island of Tsushima near Korea), and, on the other, Toyotomi lieutenant Konishi Yukinaga.

To paraphrase Sin Sukchu, Korea thus lost the means to pacify Japan. This is why Ryu Sŏngnyong, who played a very active role during the Toyotomi invasions, felt compelled to cite in the introductory chapter of his seventeenth-century book *Chingbirok* (Book of Corrections), an anecdote concerning Sin Sukchu as he lay on his deathbed. According to this anecdote, as he was departing this world, Sin, in response to an inquiry he had received from King Sejong, stated that it was his "wish that our state will remain on peaceful terms with Japan." Just as Toyotomi and the Japanese had underestimated East Asia during the invasions of Korea, so had Korea underestimated Japan.

This stance that Korea had adopted toward Japan unfortunately did not change, even after suffering the ravages of war. Roughly thirty years later, under a different set of circumstances, the Koreans would bring another disaster, of the same if not greater magnitude than the "Japanese disturbances," upon themselves.

Japan's Korean Expeditions as Seen from the Chinese Perspective

When Korea came under attack by Japan, it requested reinforcements from Ming China. As a tributary, Korea wanted China to save it during its time of crisis. In other words, Korea wanted to use its "serving-the-great" relationship with China as a means to save it from its breakdown of "neighborly relations" with Japan. Korea's once separate relationships with Japan and the Ming had now come to be inextricably intertwined.

Ming intervention resulted in Toyotomi's Korean expeditions making an indelible mark upon Chinese history as well. Indeed, the ensuing war came to be counted as one of the three major wars of the late Ming era, which are referred to by Chinese historians as the "Three Great Campaigns of the Wanli Emperor." What had begun as a war between Japan and Korea had now morphed into a war between Japan and the Ming. However, such a development arguably constituted Toyotomi Hideyoshi's original intention. He had, after all, as noted above, made clear that it was his intention to go "into China." At any rate, Ming involvement meant that a peaceful solution would require negotiations not between Korea and Japan, but between the Ming and Japan.

While the Japanese army initially succeeded in sweeping across the Korean Peninsula with great vigor, it would lose control of the sea after suffering defeat at the hands of Korean naval forces. The arrival of the Ming army also forced Japanese troops farther back, and they eventually suffered a decisive defeat in Pyŏngyang. Thereafter, a stalemate ensued, enabling the first efforts toward reconciliation to commence.

As with the campaigns themselves, the significance of these peace efforts is difficult to grasp. At a glance, the negotiations appear to have been conducted in accordance with the Ming worldview. Indeed, the debates within the Ming government at the time revolved solely around whether Toyotomi Hideyoshi ought to be invested, and whether it would be prudent to allow him to send tribute missions to the Ming. The negotiations, too, proceeded along similar lines. In other words, the Ming were deliberating whether or not Japan should be incorporated into its world order.

This central focus—of whether or not Toyotomi ought to be incorporated into the Ming world order—thus meant that none of the Toyotomi regime's plans or assertions were given concrete articulation in these negotiations. At the most basic level, Toyotomi arguably planned to first ensure that Korea submitted to Japan and, from there, to use that success as leverage for paving the way for a Japanese conquest of Ming China.

While these plans constituted a complete departure from the world order envisioned by the Ming, from the perspective of Toyotomi Hideyoshi, and possibly all of Japan, neither investiture by a Chinese dynasty nor permission to offer tribute to them would have been of any consequence.

It is unknown what Toyotomi's intentions really were. If he actually entertained the idea of conquering the Ming, then he was without doubt a megalomaniac, though such an explanation is arguably overly reductive. In any case, it is, at the very least, evident that Toyotomi's regime as a whole neither understood the Ming world order nor would be content with entering into it lightly.

But the opposite was true as well: the Ming by no means understood the Japanese stance. If the Ming thought that negotiations alone would engender a peaceful outcome, then we must conclude that they were wrong about the very premise upon which the talks had been initiated in the first place. And, in fact, there were moments of breakdown in the negotiations. Yet, somehow, they did go forward, despite these misunderstandings.

However, the peace negotiations between Japan and the Ming did finally collapse, and both sides stubbornly recommenced hostilities. The only thing that could stop the war was the elimination of Toyotomi, who was both the architect of this war and also obsessed with its conduct.

So, while the eventual death of Toyotomi Hideyoshi in 1598 did finally bring an end to the war, many of the issues raised by the Korean expeditions would remain unresolved.

For instance, while it is likely that the ideas and actions of Toyotomi were idiosyncratic, neither war nor diplomacy can be reduced to the work of a single individual. His Japanese contemporaries, regardless of their own personal feelings and thoughts, willingly accepted his cause and followed him into battle. Furthermore, they themselves were by no means removed from Toyotomi in terms of their aversion to the world order to which both the Ming and Korea subscribed.

The question of how to handle Japan was thus a difficult one for both the Ming and Korea. How could they build a relationship with a neighboring country that had suddenly risen to power in the Age of Discovery, rejected the logic of their world order, and had the potential to evolve into a major military threat? This was a question of survival for the Korean government, whose domain had been violated by the Japanese during Toyotomi's invasions, and was a question of unprecedented significance for the dynasty that governed neighboring China.

However, Japan was not the only problem that the Ming and Korea would have to contend with. While the sixteenth century concluded with the rise of Japan in "the Far East" and one of the bloodiest wars to ever be waged in human history, the seventeenth century would see the rise of another new power.

3. The Manchu Disturbances

Mongols to the North, Japanese to the South

In 1616, during the late Ming, the writer Xie Zhaozhe penned an essay titled *Wuzazu* (Five Miscellanies). The essay contains a famous passage that helps give a sense of the worldview shared by the people of the Ming dynasty at the time:

> There is no barbarian country that values decorum as much as Korea and no land more fertile than Jiaozhi [Vietnam]. There are none fiercer than the Tatars and none craftier than the Japanese. There is no place more unsophisticated than Ryukyu and none richer than Zhenla [Cambodia]. . . . It matters little to China whether other countries rebel or submit. We are concerned only with the potential threat of the Mongols to the north and the Japanese to the south. After these, the only other problem is the Jurchen.

As stated here, the late Ming was a period in which the dynasty found itself surrounded: the Mongolians ruled the north, and the Japanese the southern seas. For the Ming, Xie Zhaozhe's words helped give articulation to the threat posed by the "fierce Tatars" of the northern plains (the Mongols) and by the "crafty Japanese" in the southern seas.

Objectively speaking, however, this was a crisis that the Ming had in fact brought upon themselves.

At the basis of Ming ideology and its approach to foreign relations was the notion that a distinction existed between "civilized" and "barbaric" peoples. This binary found application in the way in which the Ming divided people and regions. For instance, they tried to physically institute this division by banning maritime activities along the long Chinese coastline, and by fortifying the Great Wall in the north that still stands today.

However, such patterns of thought and behavior were, in many ways, out of kilter with the way in which the world and China were moving in the sixteenth century. Silver was rapidly circulating around the globe, and this helped stimulate the Chinese economy and Chinese society as well. The threats that the Mongols in the north and the Japanese in the southern seas came to pose to the Ming dynasty can be understood as a kind of allergic reaction on the part of these peoples—an allergic reaction to the Ming's regulation of foreign interactions, trade, and finance, and furthermore, to the worldview that underpinned such policy.

In fact, both the Mongols and the Japanese came to clash with the Ming precisely because their desire to trade on official terms with China went unsatisfied. Because the Ming were unwilling to allow the Mongols and Japanese to engage in official trading relations with them (this was a privilege reserved for China's tributaries), the Mongols and the Japanese came to engage in overt, but unlicensed, trade with China. And, eventually, such illicit operations did become a reality. These circumstances were at the very heart of the Ming clashes with these peoples.

It is well known that the Japanese pirates were in fact made up of a variety of peoples, not the least of whom were Chinese. Exactly the same held true for the Mongols in the north. Chinese and non-Chinese were united through commerce, formed armed organizations, engaged in illicit trade, and resisted repression by the Ming authorities.

Communities also began to form along the northern borders and coastlines of Ming China—at the very boundary lines between "civility" and "barbarity"—which were centered around armed commercial groups comprising both Chinese and non-Chinese peoples. From amidst these multiethnic and multilingual communities emerged a new driving force that would shape the contours of the era to come.

But that power would be neither the Mongols of the north nor the Japanese of the southern seas. It would be those whom Xie Zhaozhe identified as the next problem with whom the Ming would have to contend: the Jurchen of the Liaodong area.

The Jurchen in the Ming Period

The Jurchen started out as a truly weak group. In population alone, their numbers were far smaller than that of the Chinese mainland to their south or even that of the Korean Peninsula.

It had been said since ancient times that the "Jurchen warriors" numbered fewer than ten thousand. Their small absolute number derives from their having been divided into smaller groups and never unified. However, as a people who lived off nomadism and hunting, their fierceness was unrivaled, and it was said that they would be "invincible if they numbered ten thousand."

The Jurchen had rapidly risen to prominence in the twelfth century, overthrowing both the Liao and Song dynasties and founding the Jin dynasty. After the Jin were overthrown by the Mongol Empire, the Jurchen reverted to a state of small separate powers. During the rise of the Ming dynasty, they submitted to the Hongwu and Yongle emperors.

The Ming geographically demarcated the Jurchen and employed a kind of indirect rule over them. Generally speaking, the Jurchen can be divided into three different groups: the Jianzhou, near the Liaodong Peninsula; the Haixi, to the north; and the Wild Jurchen, farther to the east.

Subsequently, the Jurchen came to conduct peaceful trade with the Ming and Korea, their specialty products being ginseng, pearls, and marten furs. The demand for such high-grade products soon increased steadily as an effect of the sixteenth-century Age of Discovery and the concomitant boom in commerce. What is more, the connection between the Jurchen and Japan came to be especially strong as a result of their relative geographical positions.

The Japanese silver that flowed toward the Korean Peninsula was traded for silk products, cotton goods, and other Chinese wares, some of which went to Japan in return for the silver. China, as the original exporter, naturally profited from the trade, as did the Korean Peninsula as an intermediary. This stimulated demand for Jurchen specialty products. And it stands to reason that as these trade transactions became more frequent, associated conflicts increased as well.

An inviolable rule of history in all times and places is that a powerful neighboring state is to be avoided. As long as the Jurchen were divided into small groups and remained loyal, both the Ming and Korea had peace of mind. However, they were sensitive to any signs of rebellion.

During the reign of King Sejo of the Chosŏn dynasty (r. 1455–1468), Sin Sukchu subjugated the Wild Jurchen to the north. Moreover, when the Jurchen chieftain Li Manzhu of Jianzhou rebelled against the Ming, Sejo dispatched Kang Sun and others to launch a pincer attack together with the Ming army, allowing them to capture and kill Li Manzhu. Following these events, for the remainder of the fifteenth century, the Jurchen would no longer pose a threat to either the Ming or Korea.

The Rise of Nurhaci

Yet this situation changed in the latter half of the sixteenth century. In Ming China, as the military threat of the northern Mongolians grew, smuggling increasingly thrived, and the activities of armed commercial groups became more evident in the Liaodong borderlands.

Areas under Ming control, including Shenyang, Fushun, and Kaiyuan in Liaodong, intruded like wedges into the lands inhabited by the Jurchen. This borderland, full of walls and fortresses, known as the frontier wall (C. *bianqiang*) and dividing inner from outer, became the site of repeated uprisings of large-scale warlord groups dependent on commerce. One of these warlords was Nurhaci of Jianzhou, based in the area between the Ming frontier wall and the Yalu River. He would win out against all rivals, eventually becoming the *taizu*, or founding father, of the Qing dynasty.

Nurhaci raised his army in 1583, about ten years prior to the Korean expeditions of Toyotomi Hideyoshi. He led a very small force of one hun-

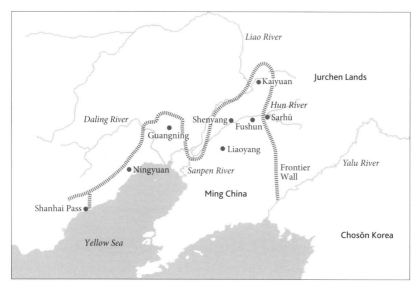

The Liaodong region in the late Ming period

dred warriors, of whom only thirty wore armor, to attack the Jurchen leader Nikan Wailan. Nikan had killed Nurhaci's father and grandfather, and had contact with the Ming army. No one at this time could have imagined that this would constitute the beginning of a chain of events that would change the course of East Asian history.

Five years later, Nurhaci had defeated almost all who had resisted him in his homeland of Jianzhou. The five tribes of Jecen, Hunehe, Suksuhu, Wanggiya, and Donggo that he united came to be collectively known as "Manju Gurun" (the Manju State). The etymological source word of this term is "Mañjuśrī," which is also the original word from which the Chinese "Wenshu Pusa" (the bodhisattva of keen awareness) is derived. "Manju Gurun" would later come to replace the term "Jurchen" as the ethnonym for these people. The word "Manchu" also derives from here.

The Ming authorities that bordered these tribes to the west did not obstruct Nurhaci's activities. They felt the best thing to do was to permit the existence of Nurhaci's power and to continue to engage with him as a stable contact for trading matters.

Li Chengliang, a major warlord who had wielded power in Liaodong for thirty years, was the principal advocate of this policy. What is more, if we look to the power dynamics in play at the time, we find that Nurhaci may well have been able to augment his power under the protection afforded by Li's backing.

Both Li's forces and Nurhaci's Manju Gurun had many traits in common. For instance, they had both emerged by riding the commercial boom in the frontiers. Both forces also constituted the type of armed commercial groups mentioned above, which were made up of Chinese and non-Chinese people alike. Moreover, they coexisted on either side of the frontier wall.

It was in this context that the Korean expeditions of Toyotomi Hideyoshi took place. Nurhaci's reaction to this war, in which Li's son, Li Rusong, fought, is not entirely clear. The only thing we know for certain is that Nurhaci offered his assistance to the Korean government but was turned down.

While this war devastated the lands of Korea and bankrupted the finances of the Ming, its effects were not wholly negative. As the Ming dispatched its troops, vast numbers of people and materials moved through the Liaodong area. Such movements likely served to further stimulate the economy there. And, with the end of the Korean expeditions and the dawn of the seventeenth century, the region would reach a major turning point.

The Emergence of the Aisin State

The Hulun branch of the Haixi Jurchen felt threatened by the rapid growth of Nurhaci's power. It was for this reason that, in 1593, they formed an alliance with the neighboring Khorchin Mongols and went to battle with him. It was Nurhaci who emerged victorious, however, defeating their 30,000-strong force. After securing this victory, Nurhaci's sphere of influence expanded even further, and he suddenly found himself on the path to unification of all the Jurchen peoples.

With this development, the Ming, having initially permitted the status quo so far as Nurhaci was concerned, had no choice but to be on their guard as well. It was, however, the downfall of Li Chengliang, who had long protected Nurhaci and maintained friendly relations with him, that ignited an irrevocable antagonism between the two sides. As a consequence of this event, the Ming treated Nurhaci as an enemy beginning in 1608, and they allied with other forces who viewed him in such terms. Even so, both parties made compromises, and relations did not break down immediately.

Meanwhile, as Nurhaci got closer to unifying the Jurchen, he also assumed a firmer stance toward the Ming. As a means to enhance profitability, he sought to monopolize the sale of ginseng and marten furs, which, as mentioned previously, were the Jurchen peoples' two major specialty products. This helped bolster his force's reputation as an armed commercial group. But disputes persisted due to these actions, as well as over Jurchen treatment of Han Chinese immigrants and the issue of border demarcation. The antagonism gradually deepened and, by the late 1610s, it was only a matter of time until open conflict would break out.

The period from Nurhaci taking up arms to his death was some forty years: forty years which were permeated by warfare. By broadly dividing the chronology of his life into the first thirty years and the final ten years, his life story becomes much easier to follow. The former was spent working together with the Ming and unifying the Jurchen; the latter was a time of open hostility with the Ming.

Nurhaci's country was called "Manju" in the former period, and "Aisin" in the latter period, especially within the context of its foreign relations. "Aisin" means "gold" in Manchu, so the convention is to refer to it as the Later Jin, to differentiate it from the Jin dynasty (the character for "Jin" also means "gold") that ruled China in the thirteenth century.

In 1616, at a point when Nurhaci had unified nearly all the Jurchen, he was enthroned as their ruler, or khan. Such an event was likely indicative of the preparations and internal unity he was seeking to build in preparation for his unavoidable confrontation with the patently antagonistic Ming.

Two years later, he determined to take on the Ming and issued a declaration to that effect. In the following year of 1619, he won a major victory

The accession of Nurhaci
Reprinted from *Da Qing Manzhou shi lu: Da Qing Taizu Gao huangdi shi lu* [Manchurian Veritable Records of the Great Qing; The Veritable Records of the Grand Founder, Emperor Gao of the Great Qing] (Taipei: Hua lian Chubanshe, 1964).

by defeating the allied armies of the Ming and Korea in the Battle of Sarhū, and swallowed up the Hulun Yehe tribe that had resisted him until the bitter end.

That was not all. Nurhaci also crossed the frontier wall and invaded the predominantly Han Chinese–inhabited lands under Ming control. And, when Shenyang and Liaoyang fell in 1621, he moved the capital to Liaoyang. It was in this way that a small armed group, which had started out by initially raising an army of just one hundred, gradually evolved to become a multiethnic state that brought both Chinese and non-Chinese together.

The Manchu Invasion of Korea in 1627
(The Later Jin Invasion of Chosŏn)

The rapid growth achieved by Nurhaci in the five years after he had become khan completely changed the power balance in the Liaodong area. Until then, the Ming and Korea had been the two major powers in the region, separated by what can be termed a no-man's-land. It was for this reason that the *zongfan* relationship between these two countries, who were unified through a common worldview and conceptualization of order, could endure untroubled.

However, the Ming-Chosŏn *zongfan* relationship would come to be fundamentally disrupted when a new power, which operated according to an alien set of principles and vision of order, emerged in the region: Nurhaci's Aisin. And, it would be the weaker Korea that, sitting in greater geographic proximity to this new power, would struggle to determine the best course of action to take under these newly emerging circumstances.

Kwanghaegun, the Korean king at the time, was acutely aware of the new set of geopolitical circumstances that were unfolding before him. It was for this reason that he attempted to court both sides in a careful balancing act. He continued to engage with the Ming according to the Confucian principles of ritual propriety, and he also sought to build amicable relations with the Aisin as well. At the Battle of Sarhū between the Ming and the Aisin, however, he would ultimately take the Ming side, dispatching ten thousand troops to aid the Ming forces. However, Kang Hongnip, the commander of this force, barely engaged in combat before surrendering to Nurhaci.

Nurhaci was a shrewd man, and found no fault in Korea for siding with the Ming. Indeed, such a decision made perfect sense. After all, the Ming constituted a powerful threat to the rising regional supremacy of the Aisin and, given both geographical and historical circumstances, it was only natural that Korea would choose to side with the Chinese dynasty. Nurhaci must also have been sympathetic to the unique set of circumstances Korea faced at the time. So long as the Aisin were engaged in conflict with the Ming, they could not afford to alienate Korea while it sat on the fence. To do so would drive Korea into the enemy's arms.

Advancing westward, in 1626, Nurhaci's forces were overpowered in Ningyuan by Ming forces who opened fire on them with Portuguese-made artillery. This was both the first and last loss for Nurhaci who had, up until this point, reaped success after success in battle. Indeed, he would fight no more battles and would die soon afterwards.

Nurhaci's successor, Hong Taiji, would face an even tougher set of circumstances. Hong's forces were militarily inferior to the Ming, and political circumstances in Korea, his neighbor to the south, changed drastically after he came to power. In 1623, Kwanghaegun was deposed in a coup d'état and replaced by King Injo. Unlike his predecessor, who had sought to remain on amicable terms with the Aisin, King Injo advocated an active policy of "repelling the barbarians" that saw the Aisin in adversarial terms. The Aisin were now facing enemies front and back.

In an attempt to overcome these trying circumstances, immediately after his accession in 1627, Hong Taiji dispatched troops into Korea. Known as the "Manchu Invasion of Korea in 1627" (or the "Later Jin Invasion of Chosŏn"), these attacks were led by Kang Hongnip and other Korean military men who had, after suffering defeat, defected to the Aisin side. Despite having previously advocated a policy that positioned the Aisin as adversaries, the Koreans were taken by complete surprise, and they suffered a harrowing defeat. King Injo, who had fled to Kanghwa Island, had no choice but to surrender. Having achieved the upper hand, it was the Aisin who unilaterally dictated the terms of peace, forcing the Koreans to engage with the Aisin as an "older brother" and exacting a promise from them to not launch any attacks.

This course of events and its outcome show how much the Aisin feared that Korea might launch a pincer attack in collaboration with the Ming. At the time, it is probable that the Aisin still had little intention of fundamentally reconceptualizing the terms by which they interacted with Korea on a bilateral level. Instead, in the face of the Ming threat, their main goal was ensuring a bright future for the Aisin regime.

However, the realization of such a goal proved to be exceedingly difficult. It became clear to the Aisin that the only way they could guarantee Korean nonaggression was by having the country move to fundamentally recalibrate the terms of its *zongfan* relationship with the Ming. While Hong Taiji himself had come to realize this, it would take roughly another ten years before he committed to taking such a step.

4. From "Civility" to "Barbarity"

The Premises of Qing-Korea Relations

With the Manchu Invasion of Korea in 1627, the relationship between the Aisin and Korea entered a new phase. While perhaps difficult for us to understand today, both parties referred to this relationship as one that was premised on "fraternal" terms.

This manner of expressing relations between two monarchs and states with the pretense of being bound by kinship or blood had been used throughout the course of East Asian history. For example, in China in the eleventh century, Emperor Zhenzong of the Song dynasty and Emperor Shengzong of the Liao dynasty came to coexist as "brothers" (with Zhenzong being the "elder brother" and Shengzong the "younger brother"). Similarly, Emperor Shizong of the Jin dynasty and Emperor Xiaozong of the Song dynasty in the twelfth century coexisted as "uncle" and "nephew."

While the former arrangement tended more toward a sense of equality and the latter a sense of inequality, both symbolized relationships of peaceful coexistence in situations when neither was able to militarily overwhelm the other. However, such familial designations only served as symbols of the relationships, and did not necessarily regulate or constitute binding agreements regarding their precise parameters of interaction. As we might expect, the relationships themselves were determined by the balance of interests and power of the parties concerned.

How, then, did such circumstances apply to the "fraternal"relationship between the Aisin and Korea? While both sides consented to using the terms "elder brother" and "younger brother," they assigned different meanings based on their respective positions, interests, and capacities. This meant that their interpretations of the terms didn't necessarily align.

This interpretive asymmetry can be gleaned from the records of the peace negotiations that followed the Manchu Invasion of Korea in 1627. There, the Aisin side stated the following:

> If Korea sincerely desires peace, then you no longer need to serve the Ming. You ought to sever that relationship and regard us, the Aisin, as your elder brother, with you yourself becoming our younger brother. Even if this were to enrage the Ming, we have nothing to fear so long as we work together as neighbors.

In response to this demand made by the Aisin side, the Koreans judged that while "the demand for us to sever our relationship with the Ming is wholly unacceptable as it goes against our moral principles," there was no need for them to dispute their "fraternal obligations" to the Aisin.

Accordingly, the Koreans sent the following reply to the Aisin:

> We have served the Ming as a subject for more than two centuries and our obligations have already been set, so how could we ever be duplicitous? Although our country is weak, we have long been known for our decorum. If we were to suddenly turn on the Ming, would not even you think less of us? The principles of serving-the-great and neighborly relations each have their place. We are presently seeking peace with you in accordance with [the principle of] neighborly relations, but we [continue to] serve the Ming because of [the principle of] serving-the-great. There should be no contradiction in pursuing both at the same time.

The Aisin side finally assented to this argument, stating:

Yours is indeed a country of decorum. It is admirable that you will not compromise on your principles even when facing a crisis such as this. If you will not turn on the Ming, then so be it.

This confrontational exchange is taken from the *Chosŏn wangjo sillok* (Veritable Records of the Chosŏn Dynasty), with the document itself being a report which the Koreans submitted to the Ming side regarding the negotiations. As such, it was an account drawn up with the deliberate purpose of arousing the sympathies of the Ming with regard to Korea's predicament.

In the report, Korea framed its "fraternal obligations" with the Aisin in accordance with the principle of "neighborly relations." Furthermore, Korea also explicitly stated that it had no intention of giving up its relationship of "serving-the-great" with regard to the Ming. In other words, the official interpretation that the *Chosŏn wangjo sillok* and, by extension, the Korean court, probably wanted to make was that Korea's foreign relations would go unchanged, and that the Aisin had acknowledged this.

At the same time, the *Chosŏn wangjo sillok* mentions that the Aisin rebuked and protested against the Koreans for using the name of the Ming era "Tianqi" in their documents. The adoption of this Ming era name was tantamount to yielding allegiance. The Aisin repeatedly demanded that the Koreans change the era name that they used from "Tianqi" to the Aisin name of "Tiancong." The issue was finally resolved when the Koreans discontinued their use of "Tianqi" and instead represented dates according to the traditional Chinese sexagenary zodiacal calendar cycle.

Naturally, no mention of this exists in the Aisin records. There, we merely find demands made of the Koreans like "envoys from the Aisin ought to be received in the same way as you receive envoys from the Ming" and statements made by the Korean king such as "it is better to interact with the nearby Aisin than the faraway Ming."

The Aisin record suggests that, from its perspective, it had insisted that Korea sever its relationship with the Ming, or, failing that, come to respect and revere the Aisin on a par with the Ming. As relayed by the *Chosŏn wangjo sillok*, such intentions on the part of the Aisin could also be gleaned from the obstinacy it displayed during its peace negotiations with Korea, when it sought to dissuade Korea from continuing its use of the Ming era name of "Tianqi." Indeed, from the Aisin perspective, the abandonment of the Ming calendar had been promised to them by Korea when they forged their new "fraternal" relationship.

The issue for us here does not lie in determining which of the records is correct. Instead, what we need to take note of is how vastly different the positions and perceptions of Korea and the Aisin were, despite having been party to the same peace negotiations, and having mutually invoked the same wording of "brothers" to describe their bilateral relationship. Evidently, a perceptual gap between their respective understandings of their "fraternal" relationship stood between them from the very beginning. Such contradictions would eventually have to be resolved.

The Founding of the Qing Dynasty and Its Invasion of Korea
Just as Nurhaci had failed to capture Ningyuan, so did Hong Taiji. Nevertheless, the Aisin continued to grow in power, with an especially significant turning point being their Mongol Expedition of 1634.

This westward expedition ended with the Chahars of present-day Inner Mongolia submitting to the Aisin. Hong Taiji, who had already become ruler of all the Jurchen peoples as well as the Han-inhabited Liaodong region, now ruled over the Mongols, too. Having become ruler to the Manchus, Mongols, and Han Chinese alike, Hong now needed a title befitting such power.

Using the imperial seal of the Yuan dynasty that he had acquired from the Chahars to style himself as successor to the Great Khan of the Mongolian Empire, Hong took on the status of emperor with the support of the Manchus, Mongols, and Han Chinese. In 1636, he gave his new domain the name of "Daicing gurun" (the Great Qing), and took the name of "Chongde" as his reign title. Thus was the Qing dynasty founded.

This process was highly significant, for it placed the Aisin, or the newly constituted Qing dynasty, on an equal footing with the Ming, regardless of actual power. In other words, it had rendered the Ming and Qing as mutually exclusive entities. The Confucian worldview posits that the emperor is the Son of Heaven and in receipt of the Mandate of Heaven. Since there was only one Heaven, there could only be one Mandate of Heaven and one Son of Heaven. As a loyal follower of this worldview, Korea was thus placed in yet another difficult position by the rise of the Qing.

At the time of Hong Taiji's imperial enthronement, the Korean position had already become a major issue. While Hong had successfully subjugated both the Mongols and the Koreans, the former wanted to endorse him as emperor, while the latter took a wholly indifferent stance.

Hong Taiji's perspective was that "the Mongols are my children and the Korean king is my younger brother." Thus, he thought it strange for them to take different actions because the Mongols and the Korean king were supposed to occupy the same position relative to him. Hong accordingly issued an order to inform the Korean king about his imperial enthronement. A joint letter was thus sent by key ministers of the Qing government together with Mongolian leaders, recommending that the Korean king "promptly dispatch a near relative of the king and join in acknowledging [Hong Taiji as emperor]."

The Aisin envoy carrying this letter arrived in Korea in the spring of 1636. When he conveyed the purpose of his visit, however, a heated debate ensued in the Korean court which ended in the letter not being accepted.

Hong Taiji was thus enthroned as emperor of the Great Qing without any form of acknowledgment from Korea. Before the end of that year, he personally led 130,000 men in an expedition to Korea in an attempt to exact its endorsement. With this, Qing-Korea relations once again broke down. The scale and destructiveness of this so-called "Qing Invasion of Korea in 1636" went far beyond that of the earlier Manchu Invasion of Korea in 1627, as did its impact on times to come.

It is claimed in the Qing records that the Qing invasion was preceded by Hong Taiji appealing to Korea to acknowledge his imperial enthronement. However, Hong Taiji himself never genuinely believed that the Koreans would acquiesce to this request.

Mongolia's acceptance of Hong Taiji as emperor had allowed it to be made a region of the Qing Empire that could operate autonomously and continue to practice its own customs and traditions, known in Chinese as a "borderland region" (C. *fanbu*). Given such events, logically speaking, one might hypothesize that had Korea, like the Mongols, agreed to acknowledge Hong Taiji as emperor, it too might have been treated in similar terms, as opposed to becoming a Qing tributary. Yet it was likely that no one at the time believed that such an outcome was possible.

It would be more appropriate to see the appeal that Hong made as a challenge to Korea to make a final decision to abandon the Ming and follow the Qing. And just as Hong expected, the Koreans declined to engage with him as the new Son of Heaven. The ensuing expedition to Korea, which Hong himself led in person, was launched with (a) a confidence that, given regional circumstances, this was the opportune moment to make such a move, and (b) the belief that given such circumstances, he could engage in a full-fledged attack upon Korea without having to worry about his home soil being attacked in the meantime.

When we consider the events of the Qing invasion of Korea together with the founding of the Qing dynasty and the imperial enthronement of Hong Taiji, it becomes clear that the historical significance of the expedition extends far beyond that of a mere expedition. Indeed, it was a challenge to both the principle of "serving-the-great," which Korea so doggedly sought to stand by, and the very world order that the Ming were so desperate to see remain intact.

What Constituted a "Fraternal" Relationship?

From the Qing standpoint, Korea had been subjugated in the Manchu Invasion of Korea in 1627. Indeed, this was declared in writing at the time of Hong Taiji's enthronement as emperor.

To Hong, it was this subjugation that embodied what a fraternal relationship meant, and thus it was only right that Korea should respect the Qing more than the Ming. As such, the Qing could argue that it was, in fact, the Korean king who had "betrayed his pledge" and had "broken the relationship of peaceful fraternal relations." After all, it was he who had refused to receive Hong Taiji's letter and who had refused to acknowledge Hong's imperial enthronement.

However, the Koreans understood this fraternal relationship according to an entirely different set of terms. For their part, the fraternal relationship was no different from their conventional form of "neighborly relations" with surrounding countries, meaning that, from their perspective, equality existed between the Qing and Korea. Hence, for the Koreans, their "serving-the-great" relationship with the Ming was something altogether separate.

The following memorandum, written by Hong Ikhan, an official at the Office of the Censor General and one of the most fervent advocates of all-out war with the Qing at the time, helps to clarify the Korean stance:

> Since being born on this earth, I have heard of no Son of Heaven other than the Son of Heaven of the Great Ming. It is absurd that those barbarians should barbarize our national customs, enslave our ruler and those he rules, and seek to become the Son of Heaven. We have long had the reputation of being a country of decorum and are known across the world as Little China. (*Chosŏn wangjo sillok*)

This sentiment was more or less shared by all Koreans.

Even so, it was not possible to simply refuse the letter and turn a deaf ear to the matter, so the Koreans did eventually send a response.

It goes without saying that they could not explicitly curse the Qing by calling them "barbarians" therein. The Qing records contain the phrase "We do not see that you intend for us to respect each other fraternally at all, but rather it was as if you were addressing a slave." The *Chosŏn wangjo sillok* contains another letter, with the passage "You also said that we are virtuous in not betraying the Ming, and therefore you have determined an agreement of neighborly relations with us." While the Qing did not accept the latter, the Korean argument was, in effect, a critique of the Qing, saying that it was *they* who had gone against the terms of their fraternal relationship.

Both the Qing and Korea adhered to the same notion of fraternal relations, but they clearly attached entirely different meanings to it.

From the perspective of the Qing, a relationship enacted on brotherly terms had proved to be insufficient for completely separating Korea from Ming influence. That being the case, the Qing had no choice but to redefine the terms of its bilateral relationship with Korea. All would have been well had Korea acknowledged Hong Taiji's imperial enthronement. However, it didn't, and the Qing had no choice but to resort to force. These were the circumstances that led to the Qing invasion of Korea.

Qing-Korea Tributary Relations

The Qing army crossed the Yalu River and surged into the Korean Peninsula from Ŭiju. It forced King Injo to surrender by surrounding him at the Namhan Mountain Fortress. When Korea surrendered, the Qing staged an elaborate performance in which King Injo personally and ceremoniously surrendered to Hong Taiji atop a high podium. The significance of this act was evident to all. The Samjŏndo Monument, which stands to this day, was erected at the site of the podium to praise the accomplishments of the Taizong emperor of the Qing and to commemorate Korea's surrender for posterity.

Then, on the 24th day of the second month of the year 1637, Hong Taiji forced his surrender conditions upon Korea. These included the severing of Korea's relationship with the Ming, replacing it with a relationship of serving-the-great with the Qing, and making it adhere to all tributary and ceremonial procedures that had applied to Korea under the Ming dynasty, including the use of the Qing calendar in all official documentation.

From the Qing perspective, Korea's submission had already taken place ten years earlier. Yet Korea had not acknowledged this submission so long as the fraternal relationship between them endured. This was the reason that the Qing compelled Korea to enter into a *zongfan* relationship with it according to a set of terms analogous to that which had previously existed between Korea and the Ming. Submission was already a reality, and this demand was intended to make Korea accept that fact.

After having entered into this new *zongfan* relationship with the Qing, the ceremonial protocol that Korea had to follow was, on the face of it, wholly identical. However, the purposes and circumstances that underpinned the performance of these ceremonies differed greatly from those which had come before.

At the time, the Ming was still a functioning and powerful dynasty. In addition, despite being compelled to enter a new *zongfan* relationship with the Qing, Korea continued to identify the Ming as *the* "superior country" that it should continue to serve. Under such circumstances, in order to both prevent Korea from rebelling and to ensure its continued subservience, the Qing could not afford to be magnanimous or lenient.

It is for this reason that, despite the superficial similarities, the *zongfan* relationship between the Qing and Korea at this time needs to be delineated from that which existed between the Ming and Korea. The Qing had to be harsh with Korea, including taking Korean royal heirs as hostages and detaining them in Shenyang, compelling Korea to present annual financial gifts to the Qing, and mandating Korean assistance in attacks launched against the Ming.

Thus, for the rest of the book, I will refer to the relationship between the Qing and Korea as a *zongshu* relationship in order to differentiate it from the *zongfan* relationship that existed between the Ming and

Korea. *Zongshu* itself is a synonym of *zongfan* used predominantly in Japanese academia. As in *zongfan*, the *"zong"* refers to the superior status of a Chinese dynasty, while the *"shu"* refers to a tributary state. Throughout the Qing dynasty, Korea continued to be referred to as a tributary (C. *fanshu*), as was the case in its relations with the Ming. However, there were other names for a tributary state as well, such as *shuguo* (J. *zokkoku*, K. *sokkuk*). Where necessary to distinguish between the Ming and the Qing, I will use *fanshu* to refer to Korea as a Ming tributary, and *shuguo* to refer to Korea as a Qing tributary.

The Course of Neighborly Relations between Japan and Korea

The conditions forced upon Korea by Hong Taiji allowed it to continue trading with the Japanese as before. However, it was also stipulated that upon receiving a Japanese envoy, the Koreans must bring him to the Qing court, as the Qing would then dispatch its own envoy to Japan. While the Qing had nothing against the exchange of envoys between the two countries, it was worried that the two might ally themselves with the Ming and seek to oust it from its seat of power. Indeed, throughout the course of the Qing dynasty, the Qing remained highly concerned about Korea's actions regarding Japan whenever events indicated that such concern might be warranted.

Korea's restoration of relations with Japan came in the early years of the Tokugawa regime, which had been established just a few years after the Japanese expeditions into Korea. In 1605, a Korean envoy was granted an audience with Tokugawa Ieyasu and his shogunal successor, Tokugawa Hidetada, at Fushimi Castle. And, in 1609, an envoy of the Tsushima Domain made his way to Korea to establish a basic set of regulations concerning interactions and trade with the country. These regulations are referred to as the 1609 Agreement.

Despite the outward appearance of such developments, the agency of the Tsushima Domain was also highly implicated in this restoration of relations. Tsushima is a Japanese island situated between Japan and Korea that had long functioned as an important trading center between the two countries. As it had very little arable land, it depended on trade with Korea for its livelihood and, following the Korean expeditions, wanted to restore interactions and trade with the country as quickly as possible. To do this, it intervened and acted as mediator for interactions between Tokugawa Japan and Korea, altering and forging state letters sent between the two. These interventions allowed Tsushima to successfully restore Japan-Korea relations.

The key target of these interventions that were enacted on the part of Tsushima concerned the title by which the Tokugawa shogun was known on an international basis. The principles of "neighborly relations" required that, as the Korean monarch was a "king," he could only ever engage with the rulers of other non-Chinese countries who were governed by an equal counterpart. To interact with a country that had a ruler of a higher status than that of "king" (i.e., an emperor) would gainsay Korea's relationship with China. In other words, state documents signed off by any other title than that of "king" could not be accepted. In the Japanese case, however, from the time of Ashikaga Yoshimitsu's rule as shogun, Japanese retainers were compelled to avoid the use of the term "king" in reference to the shogun in official documentation. To do so was considered both an act of disrespect toward the Japanese emperor and also an act of excessive deference toward the emperors of the various Chinese dynasties.

To compensate for such inconsistencies, Tsushima altered state letters as a matter of policy. Continued forgery became necessary to evade detection, and eventually became habitual.

Since Tsushima's fabrications pertained to state letters, no matter how skilled or ingenious the forgers were, the process was enacted at great risk. While the process may well have worked when Tsushima was united internally, any break in the status quo ran the risk of potential discovery and the outbreak of considerable disorder.

This would be the case some two decades later, when internecine fighting on the island came to shine a light on Tsushima's systematic forgeries and alterations of Japanese and Korean state letters. This would become a major international incident that resulted in a complete overturn of

Tsushima's position as an intermediary. Specifically, a new system was developed in which Tsushima took charge of day-to-day interactions between Japan and Korea, including that of trade, while the Edo *bakufu* took direct control of state-level affairs through its interactions with the Korean delegation to Japan. It was also at this time, in 1635 and 1636, that the shogun's international title came to be fixed as *taikun* ("great prince").

These developments coincided both with the founding of the Qing dynasty and the eve of its 1636 invasion of Korea. Arguably, the Qing's consolidation of power in the Liaodong region and the redefinition of Japan-Korea relations were not unrelated, especially with regard to the motives that governed how Korea acted in this period.

As such, while the relations between Japan and Korea in this period continued to be referred to as "neighborly relations," we nonetheless ought to differentiate them from their pre-Sengoku period counterpart. Indeed, Japan-Korea relations became far more stable than before, thanks to the establishment of the title of "great prince" for Japan's primary diplomatic representative, the establishment of a fixed diplomatic function for Tsushima, and the formularization and regularization of the dispatch of Korean diplomatic missions.

Encouraged by such developments, Korea wanted to avoid involving the Qing in its bilateral relations with Japan. Indeed, from the Korean perspective, Qing involvement could potentially further complicate and confuse matters. It was for this reason that Korea responded vaguely to any demands made of it by the Qing regarding Japan, and prevented Japanese missions from communicating with the dynasty. Instead, Korea limited its responses to the Qing to just the sharing of information about Japan.

On the Japan side, Ieyasu, too, had wanted to swiftly restore diplomatic and trading relations with the Ming. However, just several decades later, Japan had lost all desire to actively build a relationship with the ruling Chinese dynasty. Instead, Japan embraced a new policy of *sakoku* (national isolation). It was for this reason that, at least until the nineteenth century, Japan and the Qing would not come to form any kind of direct political relationship.

The Ming-Qing Transition

In 1644, the Ming were overthrown after an attack from the roving bandit Li Zicheng, who established the short-lived Shun dynasty in Beijing. Defeating Li's forces, the Qing soon crossed the Shanhai Pass, relocated their capital to Beijing, and subsequently took control of China.

Looking back, this Ming-Qing transition appears inevitable. In the years leading up to the transition, corruption was rife in the Ming government, and the Qing gradually moved to consolidate its power. The transition thus seems the natural end point for such trends. Yet for the people who lived through these tempestuous times, these developments took them completely by surprise.

The Japanese referred to the Ming-Qing transition as the "transformation from civility to barbarity." It signified that the civilized Ming had "shape-shifted" into the barbarous Qing. While this Japanese euphemism for the transition was used first and foremost to point to the dynastic shift from Ming to Qing, it also carried much deeper connotations. Indeed, the phrase also conveyed that a wholly unthinkable change to the world order had occurred, in which barbarity replaced civilization.

The phrase also gave rise to the notion that a civilized race could deteriorate into a barbarian race, and thus the notion that a barbarian race could achieve transformation into a civilized race. This latter notion shook the very foundations of the East Asian worldview and imbued the region's various ethnic groups with what one could perhaps understand as a kind of proto-nationalism. What is more, it had a major impact on the ruling ideologies of Qing China, Korea, and Japan, and stimulated the formation of a new order for the era.

During the period of Ming-Qing coexistence from 1637 to 1644, when the Ming, as a Han Chinese dynasty, firmly clung to its status as the legitimate leader of Chinese civilization, there was no greater cruelty for Korea, the self-appointed "Little China," than having to serve the barbarous Qing as its tributary. Yet what ultimately embedded that agony in Korean self-conceptions was the Ming-Qing transition itself.

While it is best to avoid counterfactual speculation, doing so can sometimes be an effective means to clarify the significance of a historical reality. If the Ming had continued as before, then the forging of the Qing-Korea *zongshu* relationship would have constituted a considerable rupture with the past. What is more, the emergence of this new relationship may have rendered the East Asian order, and the foreign relations of each of its countries, in the seventeenth century and beyond, much more complex.

The rapid Ming decline and Qing rise to power creates the illusion of a smooth transition in which Ming institutional practices passed directly, unimpeded, to the Qing. However, that was not the case. The Qing had to forge a new tributary relationship with Korea. In so doing, the Qing did not merely inherit the tributary relationship of its predecessor. It also came to use its relationship with Korea as a precedent and criterion for its forging of relations with other countries.

Additionally, with the forging of the new Qing-Korea *zongshu* relationship, the Korean royal heirs who had been held hostage by the Qing were released and sent back to Korea. Moreover, as the Qing feared attacks from maritime powers, they were content with limiting the extent of their relationships with foreign countries to tribute and trade relations, and did not actively seek anything beyond that.

All of these new circumstances were brought about because of the Qing conquest of China. However, it goes without saying that an entirely different historical outcome was entirely possible as well. It is for this reason that we need to be wary when scholars invoke such concepts as the "tributary system" to suggest that tributary relations traced a direct, contiguous, and unbroken line from the Ming into the Qing. Such interpretations are jaundiced by a preoccupation with the superficial, and a privileging of historical outcomes over historical processes.

What, then, differed between the two? The difference was the emergence of a historically unprecedented situation in East Asia following the advent of the Age of Discovery in the sixteenth century: Japan and the Liaodong area rose to prominence as political and economic powers, with the side effect that the geopolitical importance of the Korean Peninsula, which lay between them, was augmented as well.

The most eloquent testimony to this situation is the fact that the Korean Peninsula was invaded from the south in the late sixteenth century and then from the north in the early seventeenth century. There was the Japanese movement under Toyotomi and the Tokugawa, which resulted in unification and *sakoku*; the Qing movement, which resulted in the Jurchen unification, the imperial enthronement of Hong Taiji, and conquest of China; and the Korean movement, which ultimately led to the forging of peaceful relations with Japan and the Qing even as the Koreans were caught between these two expansionist regimes, insisting on their own dignity, and suffering the ravages of war.

All of these changes were an expression of the process of trial and error that was involved in determining how to settle the new circumstances of this turbulent period. The end points were the consummation of the Qing-Korea *zongshu* relationship and the restoration of "neighborly relations" between Japan and Korea. Following continuous changes in the region's geopolitical structure, the situation in East Asia was, at long last, stabilizing in the mid-seventeenth century.

In essence, the preservation of this stability depended on whether friendly relations could be maintained between Korea and the emergent powers of the Qing and Japan. Clearly, these relationships were not purely contingent upon Korea alone. Indeed, they required consent from the other parties as well. In other words, the smooth maintenance of the Qing-Korea *zongshu* relationship and Korea's "neighborly relations" not only required that Korean policies recognized and approved of the terms by which these relationships were enacted, but also required prolonged stability in the Qing rule of China and the Tokugawa rule of Japan.

That being so, neither the Qing-Korea *zongshu* relationship nor Korea's "neighborly relations" with Japan could ever become completely fixed or immutable. While these relations functioned well in times of stability, even just a short burst of instability could raise doubts about the terms and conditions upon which these relationships were built. Moreover, it was entirely possible that even when dealing with the same incident or body of text, the parties involved could bring their own unique perceptions and reasoning to bear.

This kind of interpretive plurality was already a key feature of the historical process, and could be said to have been historically instilled or to have become a historical precondition for interactions in the East Asian context.

After the period of immense upheaval described above, East Asia finally found stability in the second half of the seventeenth century. However, just two centuries later, the region would face turbulence once more.

CHAPTER TWO

The Making of "Tributary Autonomy"

1. The Eastward Advance of the Western Powers

The Workings of Japan-Korea Neighborly Relations

In the mid-seventeenth century, a new form of international order emerged in East Asia as a byproduct of the events described in the previous chapter. This new status quo, and the period for which it would endure, overlapped in temporal terms with the Edo period (1603–1868) in Japan, the latter half of the Chosŏn dynasty in Korea, and the Qing dynasty in China. Up until the mid-nineteenth century, stability prevailed across each of these regimes, allowing, for the most part, long-term stability in their trilateral relations as well. Furthermore, as had been the case previously, a variety of interactions and relationships existed within this trilateral formation. Here, I begin my discussion with the "neighborly relationship" between Japan and Korea.

In this relationship, enacted on terms of equality, day-to-day exchanges, including those pertaining to trade, were handled exclusively by Tsushima in Japan and Tongnae County in Korea. Meanwhile, governmental interactions were conducted between the envoys of the Korean communication embassies, who were dispatched to Japan at irregular intervals, and representatives of the Edo *bakufu*.

While the Koreans could travel to Edo to engage in governmental interactions, this so-called "equality" was by no means entirely equal. Indeed, if we delve deeper into the specifics of the relationship, we find further evidence of this reality. People from Tsushima who traveled to the Japan House (K. *Waegwan*) in the settlement at Pusan were, for instance, forbidden from traveling any farther into the Korean interior. Similarly, no official envoys of the Japanese government had ever been allowed to make the trip to Korea. Such circumstances were a byproduct of the suspicions the Koreans had come to harbor toward the Japanese after Toyotomi Hideyoshi's invasions. Japan-Korea exchanges were thus exceedingly one-sided.

During the Edo period, Japan functioned under what is known as the *bakuhan* system. Under this political configuration, the emperor and shogun stood side by side, making the head of state separate from the ruler. The shogun ruled over the various domains that made up the country, with daimyo, or feudal lords, representing his authority in each. This made Japan unique.

This singularity meant that Japan, in its relations with Korea (effectively the only foreign country that the Tokugawa state engaged with on a diplomatic basis) was always exposed to the latent risk of a dispute over the issue of moral obligations, such as over the relative positions of their monarchs. Indeed, it was this perceived risk that led to the forgery of state letters by Tsushima during the early Edo period. Furthermore, it was also the underlying cause for Tokugawa advisor Arai Hakuseki deliberately reviving the title of "King of Japan" at the start of the eighteenth century, to instigate a dispute with Chosŏn envoys about ceremonial receptions.

Yet this risk did not readily manifest itself. The reasons for this were that interactions between Japan and Korea were, in practice, mediated by Tsushima, and official visits from the Korean side were very limited. Such circumstances ensured that neither side was particularly knowledgeable about the other's situation.

The Tokugawa regime's introduction of the title "great prince" (*taikun*) was one illustrative example of this situation. Arai Hakuseki and Tsushima operative Amenomori Hōshū, well known for their involvement in negotiations with Korea, aptly said that, "In Korea, 'great prince' is a title conferred on a subject," while it meant "chief daimyo" (chief over all feudal lords) in Japan. Unlike "titles such as emperor, Son of Heaven, or king, that have remained constant and cannot easily be altered," the term "great prince" was capable of simultaneously accommodating a variety of meanings.

The introduction of the term "great prince" therefore allowed both the Japanese and the Koreans to interpret the word as suited them best. In the Korean context, "great prince" was a title that ranked below that of king, whereas in Japan, it was equal to or higher than that of king. Its use thus prevented either side from damaging the self-esteem of the other party. The use of the term "great prince" was just one example of the interpretive plurality that was characteristic of the Japan-Korea relationship. Indeed, many other discrepancies in perception coexisted as well. Expediently combining these and achieving coherence among them was what ensured the smooth operation of the "neighborly" relationship.

There were, of course, those who realized that these were contrivances of ignorance and misunderstanding. One of them was Arai Hakuseki. As noted above, it was he who attempted to change the title of the Japanese shogun from "great prince" to "King of Japan."

On the Korean side, we have Yi Ik, the father of the Sŏngho Practical Learning School (*sirhak*), who, a number of years later, stated the following:

The *kanpaku* [regent to the Japanese emperor] sits at the eastern extremities and has never called himself king. His title is shogun (*seii taishōgun*) [commander-in-chief of the expeditionary force against the barbarians]. . . . No more than six hundred or seven hundred years have passed since the Japanese emperor lost his power, and not all Japanese wished for that to happen. Lately, we have seen the gradual emergence of loyal men, and since "If names be correct, language is in accordance with the truth of things," I do not doubt that he will eventually regain power. If they ally themselves with the barbarians, support the emperor, and have him issue a command to all the daimyo, this may elucidate their moral duty, and I cannot imagine that anyone would go against the viceroy of all sixty-six provinces of Japan. If this were to pass, their head of state would be the emperor and ours the king, and how in the world should we handle that? . . . Back then, the chief ministers were only concerned with what was immediately in front of them, lacking any farsightedness or deep consideration. Moreover, since they did not even know that the *kanpaku* was not a king, the situation turned out as it is now. Is this not utterly deplorable? (*Sŏngho sasŏl ryusŏn* [The Humble Opines of Yi Ik Selected according to Category], 18th century)

Here, the Tokugawa shoguns are referred to as "*kanpaku*" because they inherited their status to govern Japan from Toyotomi Hideyoshi. The term "shogun" was typically reserved for descendants of the Minamoto clan, whereas "*kanpaku*" was used for members of the Fujiwara clan, of which Toyotomi claimed descendance. In writing this passage, Yi Ik demonstrated a remarkable understanding of Japan at the time: he accurately delineated the differences between emperor and shogun, demonstrated an awareness of the emerging discourse that championed imperial rule over shogunal rule, and also warned of how the situation could play out in the future.

If the Tokugawa shogun were to be overthrown and the emperor made sovereign, then his very title of "emperor" would come to present a huge dilemma for Japan-Korea relations. Indeed, the title of "emperor," by implication, surpassed that of "king," the title of the Korean sovereign. This would create a situation in which Korea's status, far from remaining equal, would drop below that of Japan's. While this fear would be realized just a century later, for the time being, those who feared such an outcome were very much in the minority.

The Workings of Qing-Korea *Zongshu* Relations

We now move on to discuss the second key relationship of the new order of the seventeenth century: the Qing-Korea *zongshu* relationship. Once the Qing had taken control of China, the particulars of the Qing-Korea *zongshu* relationship largely came to accord with the precedents established by the Ming-Korea *zongfan* relationship.

Indeed, once the threat from the Ming had dissipated, the Qing no longer feared the launching of a pincer attack backed by Korean support, and felt compelled, as successors to the Ming, to adopt a similar policy in its foreign relations. For that reason, then, just as was the case with the Ming's *zongfan* relationships, the forging of Qing *zongshu* relations, whose core practices were the receipt of tribute and return act of investiture, were by no means limited to just Korea alone. With its subjugation of former Ming territories, the Qing came to forge *zongshu* relationships with other foreign countries as well.

Even so, Korea was a special case, having entered *zongshu* relations before the Qing's ascendancy. Korea was always praised as the Qing's most obedient tributary and was always placed at the top when any lists were made of such states.

By contrast, Korea took a much more ambivalent stance toward its relationship with the Qing. While it did indeed enter into a *zongshu* relationship with the dynasty, this relationship had been forced upon it militarily. For the Koreans, the Qing still very much constituted barbarians, and relations with them were entirely undesirable. As such, Korea continued to conceptually and emotionally take pride in its self-perceived "Little China" status.

From the Korean standpoint, the civilized land once ruled by the Ming had descended into barbarity as a result of the ascendancy of the Qing. Thus, it was only Korea who was in a position to inherit the legitimacy of the Ming and Chinese civilization. Moreover, it was for this reason that Korea chose to maintain its idolization of the Ming legacy, despite that dynasty having met its downfall.

Of course, Korea was unable to display such sentiment through political action. That would be harmful and in no way beneficial to its interests. While Korean attitude and behavior toward the Qing did not quite amount to dissembling and covert betrayal, they nevertheless enacted an exceedingly pragmatic approach to the way they dealt with the Qing.

How was this pragmatism enacted? Well, Korea actively embraced relations with the Qing according to the tenets of *zongshu* relations and its own conceptualization of "serving-the-great." However, unlike its relations with the Ming, these relationships lacked sincerity. Indeed, Korea only acted in such a way to avoid incurring the wrath of Qing military incursions, out of a need to keep the country safe. These were clear-cut courses of action that were underpinned by practical considerations.

Such being the case, if the interests upon which the bilateral relationship was predicated were to change, it was likely that the Korean stance toward the Qing would shift. As we shall see, the latter half of the nineteenth century would witness just such a sea change.

Stable Relations

It was in this way that both the Qing-Korea *zongshu* relationship and neighborly relations between Japan and Korea were sustained for two centuries without any major breakdowns. The reasons Korea continued to dispatch envoys to both Qing China and Japan were twofold. Firstly, it did so as a means to preserve its amicable relations with both countries. Doing so, it hoped, would ensure Korea's prolonged safety. Secondly, it did so as a means to remain watchful of the affairs of both countries. This was due to the fact that both countries posed a latent threat to Korea's continued survival.

The envoys Korea dispatched to Qing China were called *Yŏnhaengsa*, meaning "envoys to Yanjing (Beijing)," and the records they left are collectively referred to as the *Yŏnhaengnok* (Records of Journeys to Yanjing), written between the eighteenth and nineteenth centuries. Meanwhile, the envoys Korea dispatched to Japan were the aforementioned *T'ongsinsa* (Chosŏn Missions to Japan), and they left such records as the *Tongsarok* (Records of Journeys to Edo) and the *Haesarok* (Records of Journeys across the Sea) through the thirteenth to nineteenth centuries and the seventeenth century, respectively. These extensive records are of immense historical value, for they offer a window into the contemporaneous realities of Korea's relationships with both the Qing and Tokugawa Japan. Furthermore, neither the Qing nor Japan produced sources as systematic or as complete as these on their respective relationships with Korea. The very fact that such a comprehensive source was produced in Korea, and Korea alone, speaks volumes about the Korean Peninsula's critical geopolitical position.

As for Japan and Qing China, no formal intergovernmental relations or negotiations took place between the two countries in this period. Interactions were instead limited to the unilateral trading activities of private Chinese merchants who brought their wares to the Japanese port city of Nagasaki. The trade itself was also exceedingly lopsided. While the Japanese would purchase some Chinese-made products from the Chinese merchants, these merchants shipped vast quantities of Japan's precious metals to China. Information flows were decidedly lopsided as well: while Chinese affairs might have become known in Japan, no detailed information on Japan made its way out to China. We ought to understand this to be a product of the two countries' differing economic situations and social structures, and the material and intellectual appetites they generated.

The political motivations that generated this situation between the two countries were undoubtedly a product of mutual distrust, with the Qing fearing such maritime threats as the Japanese *wokou* pirates, and Japan fearing the influx of Christian teachings. Nevertheless, given that the two countries coexisted peacefully for two centuries, their mutual policies of avoiding all unnecessary involvement between them could perhaps be said to have been sagacious.

This paucity of direct intergovernmental relations between the Qing and Japan proved to be a great boon for Korea, which, of course, engaged in both *zongshu* relations with the Qing and neighborly relations with Japan. Indeed, it enabled the country to develop these relationships free from the burden that an official Qing-Tokugawa relationship could potentially pose. This was true for Japan and the Qing as well. Their respective relationships with Korea could also continue on stable terms and take shape without either affecting the other.

The Significance of the Appearance of the West

However, history tells us that stability in relations leads both to fixed patterns of thought and to diplomatic rigidity. The two centuries of stability visited upon East Asia after the seventeenth century were more than ample to engender such circumstances in the region. By the dawn of the nineteenth century, the Western powers had changed beyond all recognition. Having undergone both civil and industrial revolutions, they began to make new inroads into East Asia. Indeed, in contrast to the rigidity in thought and action that had come to characterize East Asia, it was the outside world that made the first move in the pursuit of a dynamic new future.

That did not mean that the West played no part in the affairs of East Asia during the sixteenth and seventeenth centuries. However, for the most part, the influence of its interventions was limited to intangible economic effects, with its direct influence being little felt in political or diplomatic affairs.

As previously discussed, the rise of the Japanese archipelago and the Liaodong Peninsula was a product of a commercial boom that enveloped the whole globe, including the West. Yet the resulting political and diplomatic situation developed almost solely within the trilateral framework of Japan, the Qing, and Korea.

The exception to this was, of course, Christianity, which had a profound influence upon each of the three countries. In respect of the East Asian order, its presence was also an issue that was common to all three.

However, the influence presented by the Western advance in the nineteenth century was of a different order of magnitude from that of the seventeenth century. This is because it came to exert a direct impact not only upon the East Asian economy, but upon its various political modalities as well.

The effects that the "Western impact" had upon Japan, Qing China, and Korea were in no way uniform. The great powers naturally varied in their interests, while Japan, the Qing, and Korea were themselves swayed by their different geographic environments, economic conditions, political systems, and social structures.

An examination of the particular impacts of Western intervention in East Asia in the nineteenth century on these three countries is beyond the scope of this book. One thing that should not be forgotten, however, is that the developments that took place in Japan, Qing China, and Korea in this period were, in fact, interrelated. We also need to keep in mind that such developments brought to the surface problems that had gone unaddressed in the relations between these countries. Indeed, the nineteenth century would usher in a new phase in these countries' trilateral relations, which meant that the Qing-Korea *zongshu* relationship, the neighborly relations between Japan and Korea, and the relations between Japan and the Qing could neither continue to exist as they were nor continue to operate independently of one another.

The Transformation of the Qing Dynasty

In 1792, Great Britain dispatched its first diplomatic envoy to China. This was the Ambassador Extraordinary and Plenipotentiary Earl George Macartney. The Qing enthusiastically welcomed the mission yet treated it purely as a tributary mission, curtly turning down its request for expanded trade relations. The Qing was able to act in such a way precisely because it was the Qianlong emperor who sat at the helm of the dynasty. After all, he ruled the dynasty during its golden age. Indeed, the event was emblematic of East Asia's perceived superiority over the West at the end of the eighteenth century.

However, exactly fifty years later, in 1842, that very same Qing dynasty was subjugated by British military power and forced to conclude the Treaty of Nanking as a result of the First Opium War. It was in this way that a modern Western form of international relations, which functioned through treaty relations rather than just tribute and trade relations, was first introduced into East Asia.

Naturally, the Qing did not actively understand or seek to implement these treaty relations. This irritated the Western powers, who once more resorted to arms in 1856 in the form of the Second Opium War. Finally, in 1860, the Qing were forced to conclude a peace treaty on humiliating terms in the imperial capital of Beijing. As a result, the dynasty had no choice but to enter into the modern Western system of international relations.

A clear expression of this development came with the Zongli Geguo Shiwu Yamen (Office in Charge of Affairs Concerning All Nations), typically abbreviated as the Zongli Yamen, which was established in Beijing in early 1861.

The Treaty of Tientsin (1858) and the Convention of Peking (1860), which resulted from the Second Opium War, stipulated that envoys from the Western countries should take up permanent residence in Beijing, which made it necessary for the Qing to create a government office corresponding to a foreign ministry to deal with these envoys on a day-to-day basis. The existence and operations of the resulting Zongli Yamen thus signified how the Qing sought to interact with those countries in accordance with Western rules, albeit clumsily.

However, the establishment of the Zongli Yamen did not necessarily signify that the Qing was ready to embrace, on a wholesale level, the interstate system and form of international relations propounded by Western modernity as a new principle and criterion for its foreign interactions. From the Qing perspective, both the conclusion of treaties and the establishment of the Zongli Yamen constituted nothing more than two expedient means for averting immediate crisis and bringing the situation they faced under control.

As such, although the Qing understood and acknowledged that a treaty text bound its signatories, the dynasty did not fully accept the spirit or principles that undergirded these texts. Treaty relations were a matter that only applied to relations with Western countries. Furthermore, the Zongli Yamen was only responsible for the dynasty's dealings with Western countries. As such, neither the underlying principles of these treaty relationships nor the Zongli Yamen's jurisdictional ambit extended to regulate all of the domestic and international affairs of the Qing.

It was for this reason that, from the Qing perspective, its *zongshu* relationships with its tributaries, which predated any treaty it ever signed with a Western country, ought not be affected by any treaty or by international law. This was because the two forms of relationship were entirely separate matters that belonged to wholly different political realms.

Even so, in reality, if negotiations were, for instance, to be held between a Qing tributary and a Western country with whom the Qing engaged in treaty relations, then it would no longer be possible to regard the two types of relationship as separate matters. Such a situation would also mean that the Qing would no longer be able to stand aloof due to its involvement with both parties.

If such a situation were to come to pass, what effect would it have upon the Qing's pre-existing *zongshu* relationships with its tributaries? The answer to this question would remain unclear to all parties through the first half of the 1860s.

The Transformation of Japan

On the surface, the Japanese case followed a chronology roughly parallel to that of the Qing. Foreign ships had started coming to Japan toward the end of the eighteenth century, motivating the Edo *bakufu* to issue the Edict to Repel Foreign Vessels as a precaution. When information about the Second Opium War became known, however, the Edo *bakufu* repealed the edict and made efforts to improve relations with the Western countries.

A decade later, Commodore Matthew C. Perry arrived from the United States and forced the opening of Japan. The subsequent treaties followed more or less the same trajectory as those of China. In 1858, not long after the Qing had concluded the Treaty of Tientsin, Japan also concluded treaties of commerce with the United States, the Netherlands, Russia, Britain, and France, one after the other.

A decisive difference in the Japanese situation came with the shift in political system that occurred a decade later, after the fall of the Edo *bakufu*.

The internal developments that brought about the Meiji Restoration in Japan were the antithesis of what happened in the case of the Qing. This was because Japan aspired to become a Western-style modern state and reformed not only its domestic system of government but also its foreign relations. This sequence of historical events, while largely self-evident to the Japanese, was an exceptional development when viewed in the context of East Asia as a whole, and it was the start of something that eventually would utterly transform East Asia.

In this way, the intrusion of the West caused major repercussions for the hitherto stable East Asian order. The Qing, as a party involved in *zongshu* relations with Korea, entered into treaty relations with Western countries and began to revise its traditional model for foreign interactions. Japan, as a party involved in neighborly relations with Korea, not only concluded treaties with Western countries but also created a new political system that replaced the Tokugawa regime.

These respective developments in China and Japan shook the very foundations of the traditional *zongshu* relationship between the Qing and Korea, and the neighborly relationship between Japan and Korea. This was because the effective functioning of these relationships was contingent upon stability in Qing rule of China and Edo rule of Japan.

The French and American Expeditions to Korea

During the period in which the Qing and Japan struggled with the incursions of the West, Korea, too, faced its own set of problems, wrought by Western interference. What is more, these complications were no less troublesome than those that the Qing and Japan had to deal with. At the same time, however, in this specific timeframe of the 1860s and early 1870s, the nature of this Western interference took a very different course.

In the 1860s, a time by which the impact of the West upon Japan and Qing China had become palpably clear, Korea, too, was on the eve of a new age. In 1863, when King Ch'ŏljong died without an heir, the young Kojong of a collateral line inherited the lineage and ascended the throne, while his biological father, the Hŭngsŏn Taewŏn'gun (Grand Internal Prince Hŭngsŏn) Yi Haŭng, wielded actual power.

As imperial regent, the Taewŏn'gun implemented multifarious reforms, enforced official discipline, and significantly bolstered government authority. His strong leadership also came to be applied to the context of foreign relations, but in this regard his focus was wholly directed toward "expelling barbarians."

Since the first arrival of Christianity and Catholics in Korea, via China, at the end of the eighteenth century, the Korean government had viewed the religion and its practitioners as repudiating the ethics and rituals that underpinned their neo-Confucian state ideology. This was why the Korean government had repeatedly treated Christians with suspicion and sought to suppress their activities. This ideology, which sought to preserve the orthodoxy of neo-Confucianism and to repel the heterodox teachings of Catholicism, was called *Wijŏngch'ŏksa* in Korean.

The Taewŏn'gun likewise promoted this same movement as a way to gain ideological control. In 1866, he initiated a major suppression of Catholicism, which resulted in the execution of nine French priests who were hiding in the country, as well as thousands of Korean Christians. It is known as the *Pyŏngin saok* (Persecution of 1866).

There was a reason for this suppression occurring on such an unprecedented scale. The recent Second Opium War in China and the defeat the Qing had suffered had greatly shocked the Korean court. Envoys dispatched from Korea had witnessed both the invasion of Beijing by the British and French allied forces and the Qing emperor's flight to Rehe. The information these envoys brought home with them fueled the suppression.

The Taewŏn'gun was said to have feared that "the Rehe calamity will befall us as well" unless Christianity was suppressed. Moreover, it was not only Christianity that was identified as a target for the rejection and persecution of heterodoxy. Rather, the West as a whole also came to be viewed with trepidation and hostility. At a time when the Qing was beginning to embark on a policy of conciliation with the West, Korea was conversely becoming increasingly hostile to those same Western powers.

The French priests who escaped this crackdown reported the persecution to the French diplomatic authorities. In response, in July 1866, Henri de Bellonnet, French chargé d'affaires in Beijing, ordered the French fleet commander Pierre-Gustave Roze to lead his warships in a punitive campaign against Korea. Roze occupied Kanghwa Island in September of that year, demanding the punishment of those who had killed the priests and the conclusion of a treaty. The French were defeated in battle at various locations, however, and withdrew.

Around the time of the French invasion, an American commercial steamer, the *General Sherman*, made its way up the Taedong River, opening fire in a bid to force Korea to open its doors to trade. The Korean official in charge was Pak Kyusu, inspector for P'yŏngan Province. Assuming collective leadership over the military and civilians alike, Pak burned and sank the boat, killing everyone onboard. These French and American invasions are collectively known as the Western Disturbances of 1866.

Taewŏn'gun (1820–1898), father of King—later Emperor—Kojong
Painting by Yi Hanchol et al., Chosŏn (1869), National Museum of Korea, Seoul.

When Frederick F. Low, American minister in Beijing, heard about the loss of the *General Sherman*, he headed for Korea with a fleet of five warships in April 1871. Upon arrival, he demanded reparations for the damage and the conclusion of a treaty. As this did not work out, Low ordered his fleet to land on Kanghwa Island. While the American fleet was able to occupy some forts, the Koreans' tenacious resistance forced the Americans to withdraw after only a month. This was the so-called American Expedition to Korea of 1871.

The successful repelling of the French and American fleets fueled the Taewŏn'gun's confidence in his policy of "expelling the barbarians."

Across the country, he erected *Ch'ŏkhwabi* monuments (monuments rejecting peace) with inscriptions stating that those who do not fight "the barbarian invasion" were the same as "traitors to the nation," thereby displaying his accomplishments and resolve.

Implications for Qing-Korean *Zongshu* Relations

Tracing the course of events in this manner makes it appear as though the French and American expeditions to Korea had involved only these three countries. However, this was not the case: the Qing was heavily implicated as well due to its engagement in diplomatic relations with both France and the United States and its *zongshu* relationship with Korea. And it was the existence of this *zongshu* relationship that constituted the reason for both France and America choosing to first discuss the matter of punitive action for Korea with the Qing before launching the expeditions themselves.

It was during these discussions that both France and the United States argued that the Qing must bear responsibility for any act committed by Korea, as it was a Qing tributary (C. *shuguo*, K. *sokkuk*). However, once negotiations with the Zongli Yamen started, the response of the Qing was that Korea, although certainly a tributary of the Qing, did no more than offer tribute, and exercised autonomy (C. *zizhu*, K. *chaju*) in "all its domestic affairs."

Both de Bellonnet and Low opted for direct action against Korea on the basis of this response. Low, even more explicitly, expressed the position that Korea was "substantially an independent nation" and that, while it might send tribute to China, "there seems to be no connection between China and Corea."

However, Korea did not agree with the view of the Qing and the great powers. Korea's argument for rejecting the French and American treaty overtures derived precisely from its status as a tributary of the Qing.

The Korean argument was this: there was no way that as a Qing tributary, Korea, and by implication, the Korean king, as a subordinate subject of the Qing emperor, could engage in relations with other countries on its own accord with disregard for the suzerain authority of the Qing and its emperor, who was the Son of Heaven, and a lord and paternal authority as far as Korea was concerned. Of course, such rhetoric most likely only constituted Korea's public position, and we should not take it at face value. Rather, Korea's true position was that it hoped for Qing protection against the threat posed by France and the United States.

This must have been apparent to the Qing as well. The assertion that Korea exercised autonomy in all its domestic affairs did not, at the time, constitute an erroneous statement. However, as one might expect, there were reasons for the Qing intentionally putting this point in print. First, unless the reality of Korean autonomy was made explicit, the Western countries would struggle to comprehend the particulars and contemporary realities of what encompassed a Qing tributary or *zongshu* relationship. Second, the Qing did not want to be dragged into needless complications.

The essence of the situation was that the Qing and Korea were each trying to task the other with the responsibility and burden of dealing with the West. This suggests the solemn fact that the Qing and Korea perceived their *zongshu* relationship in different ways. Indeed, Qing-Korean relations were no longer clearly defined, a fact that had been brought to the fore as a result of the Western Disturbances in Korea. What is more, it was evident that the bilateral relationship between the Qing and Korea had now been thrown into disarray due to the new relationships these countries were beginning to forge with the Western powers.

These mutually contradictory assertions that emanated from the Qing and Korea on the nature of *zongshu* relations perplexed the Western powers, who had instigated these new shifts in regional interstate relations in the first place. Indeed, they could not invest their trust in either country's assertion. And, as we shall see, this state of perplexity over the precise terms of these *zongshu* relationships would continue for many years to come.

2. The Beginnings of Korea's Treaty Relations

From the *Shokei* Issue to the Treaty of Kanghwa

Around the time that Qing-Korean *zongshu* relations had begun to falter following the French and American expeditions to Korea, Japanese-Korean relations were likewise confronting a crisis.

Having effected the Meiji Restoration, Japan notified Korea about its restoration of imperial power at the end of 1868. However, since the document that was used to communicate this change in political system used characters such as *kō* (K. *hwang*), which means "emperor," and *choku* (K. *ch'ik*), which means an "imperial order," with respect to the Japanese emperor, the Koreans determined that such deviations from earlier epistolary protocol were haughty and rude, and so refused to accept the document. Indeed, as a participant in *zongshu* relations, Korea regarded characters like *hwang* and *ch'ik* as applicable only to the Son of Heaven, meaning the Qing emperor. For Japan, a supposed equal, to use such characters was tantamount to styling oneself as superior to Korea and constituted a negation of the bilateral neighborly relationship. The danger that Yi Ik had feared had finally come to pass.

It was in this way that the inchoate Meiji state thus came to instigate its first dispute with its neighbor, Korea. This document itself was referred to as a *shokei* (K. *sŏgye*). The incident is accordingly known as the *shokei* issue.

The *shokei* issue was an intractable one because it held implications for the divergent forms of interstate relations to which both countries were committed. Having undergone a complete overhaul of its political system, Japan was seeking to do away with the past and forge new international relationships that were predicated upon the principles of Western European diplomacy. Meanwhile, Korea sought to remain bounded by the traditional forms of interstate relations it had long been engaged in with its neighboring countries. Japan could not easily compromise, as the matter was connected with the designation of its sovereign: the emperor. Moreover, in Korea, the Taewŏn'gun government insisted upon the maintenance of its traditional form of foreign relations and remained committed to its project of "expelling the barbarians." These contradictions made the bilateral situation all the more difficult.

Five years later, the deadlock was finally broken. The Taewŏn'gun retired in 1873, after which King Kojong assumed direct rule and the Min clan, who were relatives of the queen, came to wield power. With this, the negotiations with Japan started to take a more productive turn.

Yet such developments did not mean that Korea had come to abandon its stance toward the maintenance of its traditional neighborly relations with Japan. As such, the Japanese-Korean negotiations that began in 1875 soon resulted in a new disagreement about the use of the terms "Great Japan" and "His Imperial [Japanese] Majesty" in the Japanese *shokei*. The discussions once again foundered as a consequence.

Frustrated with the situation, Japan decided to make a show of force with its warships. Japan sent the *Un'yō* into the waterways at Kanghwa Island. The ship was bombarded by the Koreans, giving the Japanese an ideal pretext to try to force a Korean reception of the *shokei*. In addition, the Japanese also used the incident as leverage to commence treaty negotiations with the country in January of the following year. The result was the signing of the Japan-Korea Treaty of 1876, also known as the Treaty of Kanghwa.

Japanese and Korean Perceptions

The actions Japan took, culminating in the the signing of the Treaty of Kanghwa, constituted an attempt to reform its traditional neighborly relations with Korea according to the principles of modern Western treaty relations. The aim of Japan was twofold. First, it intended to abolish what it saw as the "ambiguously defined private diplomacy" conducted in the day-to-day interactions of Tsushima and Korea. And second, it meant to establish modern diplomatic relations with Korea through the conclusion of a treaty between the two governments.

In order for Japan to achieve this latter aim, both countries had to subscribe to the underlying principles of sovereign statehood. It was for this reason that Japan took a great interest in the quandary that was Korea's international status. Korea's *zongshu* relationship with the Qing was hugely implicated in the issue, as were the reasons that underpinned the *shokei* issue. And, as was the case with the Western countries that had instigated the Western Disturbances in Korea, Japan, too, came to have misgivings about the facts of the Qing's *zongshu* relationships. In the words of Japanese diplomat Hirotsu Hironobu, who took part in the negotiations with Korea, Japan felt the need "to gauge the depth and solidity of the trust and protection present in the relationship between the Qing and Korea."

But in order to achieve such a determination, Japan had to choose between regarding Korea as an independent country, which was "capable of deciding all domestic and international political matters at its own discretion," or seeing it as a tributary that "relied on the Qing in all matters." Conversely, the idea that Korea was a tributary, yet exercised autonomy in all its domestic affairs (a statement that, as we saw above, the Qing had already conveyed to France and the United States), was almost unheard of in Japan at the time.

As such, the wording in Article I of the Treaty of Kanghwa of "Chosen [*sic*] being an independent state" that "enjoys the same sovereign rights as does Japan" was an assertion, so far as Japan was concerned, that indicated that Korea was not a Qing tributary but an equal and autonomous state—at least in its relations with Japan.

By contrast, the Korean government had by no means desired to conclude the Treaty of Kanghwa. It had been an unavoidable response to Japanese military intimidation.

However, these Japanese-Korean negotiations differed from, say, those with the United States, as the Koreans had not explicitly argued that their country was both a tributary of and under the protection of the Qing. In doing so, Korea was, in other words, exercising the "autonomy" that was granted to it in its internal and external affairs as a tributary, and it was precisely this "autonomy" that the Qing had referred to in its previous discussions with the French and Americans. While the Japanese had suspected that Korea might "request the Qing's protection out of fear of external pressure," such a scenario never played out.

Ultimately, Qing-Korean *zongshu* relations did not have any direct or concrete effect upon the Japanese-Korean negotiations. And, as a result, the Treaty of Kanghwa was successfully concluded between the two sides, and the text of Article I of the treaty was worded the way we saw above.

Even so, this outcome did not mean that the Korean perception was fully aligned with that of Japan. Indeed, Korea eventually acceded to the signing of the Treaty of Kanghwa not because it saw the treaty as the beginning of a new form of international relationship with the country, but rather because it understood the treaty as implying the restoration of the two countries' traditional form of neighborly relations, which had been defunct since 1868.

For instance, the meaning of the words "independent state" and "same . . . as . . . Japan" found in Article I of the treaty by no means contradicted the Korean notion of neighborly relations. This interpretation also reveals that the Koreans intellectually processed even a reorganization of its bilateral relationship with Japan according to the terms of its traditional framework.

Although Japan and Korea agreed on the same treaty and the same text, the intentions underpinning their respective decisions to do so were already far removed from each other. This is one reason for interactions between the two not being reestablished particularly smoothly between the conclusion of the Treaty of Kanghwa and the outbreak of the Imo Incident.

The Sino-Japanese Treaty of Amity, the Taiwan Expedition, and Korea

Given the troublesome interactions involved, the Treaty of Kanghwa signed between Japan and Korea cannot be considered without reference to the existence of the Qing or Qing-Korean *zongshu* relations. This raises the question of Qing interest in Japanese-Korean relations.

In short, the Qing's view of Japan, especially during and after the 1860s, consisted solely of Japan being a military threat. Broadly categorized, there were three components at play here. The first was the historical memory of the Japanese pirates; the second was the rapid Westernization on the part of Japan at this time, particularly in terms of its modernization of arms; and the third was the geographic position of the Japanese archipelago. The opinion of the Zongli Yamen was as follows:

> The Japanese were pirates in the Ming era, bringing disaster not only to the shores of Jiangnan and Zhejiang, but also to Korea. In recent years, Japan has been defeated and roused by Britain and France, and is making military preparations. If Britain or France attacks, the aim would be no more than trade or proselytization, whereas in the case of Japan, it might be conquest. If Korea is occupied by Japan, the effect on Qing security would be grave as well, and the calamity thus unleashed would be far greater than that of the French expedition to Korea. (*Qingji Zhong-Ri-Han guanxi shiliao* [Sources of Sino-Japanese-Korean Relations in the Late Qing Era], 20th century)

Here, it is important to note how the Zongli Yamen emphasized the significance of the Japanese threat and its three components for a potential invasion of Korea.

Whether the way in which the Zongli Yamen, and by extension the Qing, perceived the Japanese threat concurred with the objective reality of the situation is not what is at issue for us here. Rather, what is important is that this was how the Qing perceived Japan at the time, and that this view remained largely the same in the ensuing years as well.

In September 1871, the Qing concluded the Sino-Japanese Treaty of Amity with Japan, the first modern treaty to be signed between two Asian powers. The treaty also garnered much attention for its equal terms, which were a world apart from the terms of the unequal treaties the two powers had previously signed with Western countries. However, from the perspectives of the cosignatories, the treaty was significant for an entirely different set of reasons.

For Japan, which had initiated the treaty negotiations, its interest was first and foremost in establishing treaty and diplomatic relations with the Qing, with whom it had not previously engaged with in any substantial form of intergovernmental exchange. Particulars aside, in order for Japan to achieve its goal of becoming a modern Western-style state, a reorganization of its modes of foreign interaction was absolutely essential.

By contrast, the primary motivation for the Qing's engagement in these treaty negotiations was its aforementioned wariness of Japan. Indeed, its primary purpose was in "manipulating" the military threat that was Japan into a more amenable and less hostile state. During negotiations, the Qing were also exceedingly careful in their handling of the Korean question, which was highly important to them.

In Article I of the finalized Sino-Japanese Treaty of Amity, it states, "In all that regards the territorial possessions of either country the two Governments shall treat each the other with proper courtesy, without the slightest infringement or encroachment on either side, to the end that there may be for evermore peace between them undisturbed." At first glance, this item appears to be simply about mutual nonaggression, but this language was included at the request of the Qing, and its real aim was to forestall a Japanese invasion of Korea. This was because "the territorial possessions" (C. *suoshu bangtu*, J. *shozoku no hōdo*) of the Qing did not, from the Qing perspective, refer to just the territories under its rule, but also to its tributaries, such as Korea, over which they exercised no direct control.

Japan, of course, neither noticed this aim nor understood its implications. It was for this reason that official Qing-Japan relations, of which this treaty constituted the starting point, would soon come to be mired in trouble.

The Taiwan Expedition and the Treaty of Kanghwa

The primary example of how trouble came to beset the Qing-Japan relationship after the signing of the Sino-Japanese Treaty of Amity came with the Taiwan Expedition of 1874. Arguing that the Qing were not taking responsibility for an incident in which Ryukyuan castaways were killed by Taiwanese natives, Japan decided to invoke military force.

This expedition came as a great shock to the Qing authorities. This was because they interpreted the action not only as a tangible manifestation of the Japanese military threat that they had feared for some years, but also because Japan's sending of troops to Taiwan stood "in contravention" of the two parties' agreement to not violate "the territorial possessions of either country" as per the Sino-Japanese Treaty of Amity. With this, the Qing had now come to be apprehensive about the binding force of the treaty.

The Qing promptly set about instituting military countermeasures, moving to build a navy and bolstering its maritime defenses, on the assumption that Japan was a potential enemy. Qing fears over the future of the Korean Peninsula were also deeply implicated in these developments, motivating the Qing in the same way as the negotiations for the Sino-Japanese Treaty of Amity.

During the Taiwan expedition, the Qing were wary that Japan might also invade Korea, and notified the Korean government of this concern. This information served as part of the reason for the Korean government deciding to commence negotiations with Japan in 1874.

In this way, amid an amplification of the Japanese threat and deepening Qing worries about the Korean Peninsula, the Treaty of Kanghwa was soon to be concluded between Japan and Korea. With respect to Korea's signing of the treaty, the Qing expressed the sentiment that it was up to Korea to decide whether to conclude a treaty with Japan, and refrained from any overt intervention.

This Qing policy of non-interference was analogous to the stance it had taken to the French and American expeditions to Korea. However, at the same time, a decided shift had occurred in how the Qing perceived events this time.

The Qing perception of unfolding events can be understood as consisting of three overlapping strands, each feeding into the others. First, the Qing believed that they themselves lacked the military preparedness to resolutely commit to a "rescue" of Korea, as "had been done during the Ming." Second, the Qing believed that Japan "would not resort lightly to the exercising of military force," and would not engage in blatant acts of hostility. Third, the Qing believed that Korea's "submission" to the dynasty "came from a place of true sincerity."

It was these very perceptions that led the Qing to state to Korea that it would leave decisions of a political and diplomatic nature to Korea's discretion, while at the same time advising that Korea "endure its indignation" and seek a peaceful compromise with Japan. Given that it was these perceptions that led the Qing to advise Korea in this way, it followed that if one of the three aforementioned components changed, its stance toward Japanese-Korean relations could shift as well.

Despite the existence of the Qing-Korea *zongshu* relationship, the Qing authorities had not, in the first place, received any information from Korea regarding the details of its relationship with Japan. It was not until October 1874 that the Qing was first informed about the *shokei* issue and other disagreements that had occurred between the two countries in the past. Since the Qing was apprised of this information only immediately prior to the commencement of negotiations between Japan and Korea, it would be fair to say that the Qing was decidedly uninformed about the subtleties of Japanese-Korean relations at this time.

Objectively speaking, the Qing perspective on Japan and Korea had been overly optimistic. While viewing Japan as a threat to the

Korean Peninsula, the Qing nevertheless deemed that Japan "would not resort lightly to the exercise of military force." What is more, it had evaluated Korea's position as both "submissive" and "sincere" in its stance toward the dynasty. By the time the Qing had realized that this optimism was entirely misplaced, its vision for *zongshu* relations and Korean "autonomy" had, once again, become an issue of great magnitude, and Qing-Korean relations had become inextricably intertwined with the issue of Japanese-Korean relations.

From Shock at the Ryukyu Annexation to the Policy Advice for Korea of Concluding Treaty Relations with the West

The Qing's growing sense of crisis with regard to Japan reached a peak with the Japanese annexation of Ryukyu in 1879. From the Qing perspective, this incident, in which Japan abolished the Ryukyu Domain and established Okinawa Prefecture in its place, constituted both the "downfall" of Ryukyu, a Qing tributary, and the dissolution of the Qing's traditional *zongshu* relationship with the country.

The downfall of Ryukyu itself was not necessarily important to the Qing. Rather, what worried the Qing about Ryukyu's "downfall" was the potential precedent it set for its other tributaries. Indeed, there was a real fear that the loss of Ryukyu could catalyze a domino effect that would result in the dissolution of the Qing's other *zongshu* relationships.

In addition, the Japanese annexation of Ryukyu rekindled Qing fears over the threat Japan posed to the Korean Peninsula, albeit much more urgently this time. In more concrete terms, the Qing perceived that there was a very real danger of Japan attempting an annexation of Korea as well. The Qing had been misled by past optimism, and now needed to devise a new strategy for keeping Korea safe from potential Japanese incursions.

It was then that the Qing government hit upon a new solution for preventing Korea from "following the same path as Ryukyu": have it conclude treaties with Western countries. The idea was that if Korea concluded treaties with the Western powers, this would render Japanese interference difficult, for Japan would hesitate to intervene out of respect for the other powers. Once this plan had crystallized, the Zongli Yamen promptly entrusted Li Hongzhang, superintendent of trade for the northern ports, with the task of persuading the Korean government to begin concluding such treaties with the Western powers.

Li Hongzhang (1823–1901), Qing superintendent of trade for the northern ports
Photo from Kyodo News

Yet the maneuvering of Li Hongzhang did not yield any satisfactory results, partly because the Qing contact in Korea, the senior Korean statesman Yi Yuwŏn, opposed the signing of treaties with Western countries. Even after a year, the Korean government did not show any eagerness to pursue such diplomatic ties.

It would take a different strategy to persuade the Koreans to change their minds. This came about after Friendship Envoy Kim Hongjip, who went to Japan to engage in negotiations with the Japanese government, brought home a pamphlet entitled *Chaoxian celüe* (Strategy for Korea) in early October 1880.

Chaoxian celüe was written by Huang Zunxian, who worked at the Qing legation in Japan. In addition to offering a discussion on Korea's position in global politics, it recommended that the Korean government move to reform relations with the Qing, improve relations with Japan, and conclude a treaty with the United States. If we look at the original text, we find that the specific wording it used to convey these policy suggestions was as follows. On China, it stated that Korea should "amend, if only slightly, one's policy of the past," so as to "engage on a deeper level of intimacy with China." On Japan, it stated that Korea should "link with Japan" by "promptly revising the stipulations [laid out in the Kanghwa Treaty]." And, on the United States, it stated that Korea should "ally with the United States" by "swiftly concluding a favorable treaty."

Toward the end of 1877, the Qing dispatched He Ruzhang, minister in residence in Japan, to engage in negotiations with the Japanese government. It was, of course, He Ruzhang's most important mission at the time to conduct negotiations about the Ryukyu annexation. Given that the Qing saw the Ryukyu annexation as inextricably linked to the Korea question, it was important for them that He Ruzhang contemplated the matter in a personal capacity as well.

An important moment in this regard would come in 1880, when U.S. Navy commodore Robert W. Shufeldt and Korean friendship envoy Kim Hongjip arrived in Japan at approximately the same time. He Ruzhang took this opportunity to try informally to persuade the Koreans to conclude a treaty with the Americans.

Persuasive Opinions: *Chaoxian celüe* and *Zhuchi Chaoxian waijiao yi*

As part of He Ruzhang's plan to persuade the Koreans to enter into treaty relations with the West, he had his subordinate Huang Zunxian pen the *Chaoxian celüe* and had Kim Hongjip take it back with him to Korea. He Ruzhang met with Kim on multiple occasions, and also produced his own set of policy recommendations on the matter for the Qing government in this period. This document was titled *Zhuchi Chaoxian waijiao yi* (On the Management of Korea's/Chosŏn's Foreign Relations, 1881). When read together with the *Chaoxian celüe*, the two documents offer us an insight into the overall vision the Qing legation in Japan had for Korea's future.

In short, the main point that He Ruzhang sought to argue in his policy recommendations was that Korea, after having been rendered, in legal terms, subordinate to the Qing, should be forced to conclude a treaty with the United States. This policy was therefore advocating that Korea should be stripped of the "autonomy" that it had enjoyed in its internal and external affairs as a Qing tributary, and converted to what was known in international law as a "dependency," or "vassal state." Under this configuration, the Qing would be able to take on a more interventionist role in Korean affairs. He Ruzhang referred to this recalibration of Qing-Korean relations as "amend[ing], if only slightly, one's policy of the past," so that Korea could "engage on a deeper level of intimacy with China." As we have seen, this was the exact same expression that was used in Huang Zunxian's *Chaoxian celüe*. However, although the *Chaoxian celüe* pamphlet contained this same wording, it did not offer a concrete explanation of what was meant by these words, perhaps because it was drawn up with the intention of being shown to Korea.

Despite these efforts on the part of He Ruzhang, neither the Qing, nor the Zongli Yamen, nor Li Hongzhang adopted his policy recommendations. This was because they were aware that the adoption of such a policy came with the risk of triggering needless conflict with Japan, Korea, and Western countries, and that the dynasty was ill prepared to handle such a possibility. Thus, He's policy was disregarded.

Meanwhile, King Kojong and his close aides, having received the *Chaoxian celüe* via Kim Hongjip, were quite shocked by some of the warnings the pamphlet made about the potential for imperial incursions by a foreign power. This concern was borne out with the Min regime's introduction of modern armaments and technologies toward the end of 1880. It also followed the advice tendered in the *Chaoxian celüe* pertaining to Korea's foreign relations, choosing to embrace a policy of concluding a treaty with the United States.

In opposition to this policy, the landed *yangban* aristocrats, who had expanded their power bases since the rule of the Taewŏn'gun, once again issued a clarion call for the defense of the neo-Confucian orthodoxy and the continued rejection of the heterodoxy of Western ideas. Outspoken criticism was leveled against the *Chaoxian celüe* and Kim Hongjip, who had brought the pamphlet back to Korea. Yet, the Korean government pushed past this strong domestic opposition and moved to conclude a treaty with the United States.

Despite its embrace of the *Chaoxian celüe*'s policy recommendations, Korea had by no means completely grasped the full scope of the Qing Tokyo legation's vision for the country's future. Above all else, the

Koreans misinterpreted the meaning and implications of the wording "engage on a deeper level of intimacy with China." This was perhaps a natural outcome, given that the *Chaoxian celüe* was not specific on this point. If the Koreans had grasped the full implications of this aspect, then their stance vis-à-vis the Qing might, at the time, have undergone a complete volte-face, and history may have taken a different course.

However, the reality was that the Korean government interpreted the policy advice of "engag[ing] on a deeper level of intimacy with China" as a suggestion that the country ought to expand its interactions with the Qing. Indeed, its interpretation was utterly devoid of any sense of needing to qualitatively reform its traditional relationship with the Qing. This remained the case when the country eventually came to conclude its treaty with the United States.

The Issue of "Tributary Autonomy"

The negotiations for a Korean treaty with the United States began in earnest toward the end of 1881. Kim Yunsik, third minister of the Korean Board of Personnel, traveled to Tianjin as the leader of a student delegation and met with Li Hongzhang. Here, Kim suggested to Li that Korea might enter into treaty relations with the United States, which served as the catalyst for beginning the negotiations. From this point onward, the Qing handling of the Korea question would devolve almost exclusively to Li Hongzhang.

As a result of discussions between Li Hongzhang and Kim Yunsik, it was decided that the actual treaty negotiations with the Americans would be held in Tianjin under Li Hongzhang's leadership, while the treaty proposal assembled there would be signed in Korea. The two also drew up and agreed on the terms of a Korean treaty draft. The English version of Article I declared, "Chosen [*sic*], being a dependent state of the Chinese Empire, has nevertheless hitherto exercised her own sovereignty in all matters of internal administration and foreign relations." Let us call the idea explicated here "tributary autonomy" (J. *zokkoku jishu*). However, when referring to the Western perspective on this particular concept, I will draw upon the language used in the English version of the Article, and refer to it as "dependent sovereignty." At any rate, it was in this way that the Qing and Korea showed an apparently united front as they moved toward the conclusion of a treaty with the United States.

Korea's "tributary autonomy," as so outlined in Article I of the proposed treaty draft, was faithful to the views about Korea's status that had been previously expressed by the Zongli Yamen and Li Hongzhang. However, it is important to note here that Li Hongzhang himself had a particular reason for deliberately including this wording in the treaty text.

As was clear from the French and American expeditions to Korea, the logic that underpinned traditional tributary, or *zongshu*, relations was not understood by the Western countries. What is more, in the 1880s, these traditional forms of relationship were not only inadequately understood by the Western powers, they also ceased to be respected by them. Indeed, at around the same time that the Qing suffered the bitter ordeal of Japan's annexation of Ryukyu, Qing relations with France started to deteriorate over Vietnam as well.

Under such circumstances, the Qing had to make sure that Korea acknowledged that it was a tributary of the Qing. This was the key reason for the Qing seeking to specify the nature of Qing-Korean relations in a treaty, which would also be binding for the Western cosignatory.

The reasons that lay behind Kim Yunsik and the Korean side's acceptance of this wording pertaining to Korea's "tributary autonomy," however, did not necessarily match those of Li Hongzhang. Let us take a look at Kim Yunsik's opinion as described in his diary, the *Ŭmch'ŏngsa* (19th century):

Everyone in the world knows that Korea is a tributary of the Qing . . . Now the Qing proclaims this to all nations and declares it in a treaty. Thus, if Korea is to face an emergency in the future and the Qing do not come to our rescue with all its might, the Qing shall be the laughingstock of the world. If other countries see the Qing holding us up, they surely will not take us lightly anymore. Moreover, the [treaty] text goes on to say that [Korea is] "autonomous in all its affairs." This means that we may engage with other countries according to the principle of "the right of equality." We will not risk losing these rights, nor will we abandon our duty of serving-the-great.

This entry in Kim's diary helps to reveal the Korean perspective of what constituted a "tributary" and what form its "autonomy" took. Namely, Korea, as a "solitary and weak" tributary, was entitled to the protection of its suzerain, the Qing. Furthermore, this "autonomy" entailed that Korea could independently interact with other countries due to "the right of equality."

Thus, each concept was associated with a different party. The Korean stance was that Korea was equally "autonomous" in relation to Japan and the Western countries, and it expected the Qing to protect Korea and support its autonomy. Furthermore, it was only insofar as this applied that Korea was a Qing tributary. It can be said that Korea's traditional, pragmatic *zongshu* relations with the Qing applied to its status as a "tributary," while its neighborly relations that had been revived with the Treaty of Kanghwa corresponded with its "autonomy."

The Qing and Korean positions that were summarized in the treaty draft, which superficially appeared to coincide, thus contradicted one another.

The Qing simply wanted to demonstrate to other countries that a special relationship existed between itself and Korea, and particularly sought to emphasize that Korea was a Qing tributary. Meanwhile, the Korean side sought to stress that the Qing had allowed Korea to be autonomous and that this autonomy served as the basis for its equal relations with other countries. Likewise, the idea of "tributary autonomy" was a concept that embodied different intentions for each party. This discrepancy was bound to be exposed sooner or later.

3. The Year 1882

The Diplomatic Mission of Ma Jianzhong

Negotiations between U.S. plenipotentiary commodore Shufeldt and Li Hongzhang commenced on March 25, 1882. The biggest point of contention in those negotiations, in which no agreement was ever reached, was the aforementioned Article I that declared the tributary autonomy on the part of Korea. This was because Shufeldt maintained to the last that such terms were unsuitable for a Western-style treaty, disagreeing with the incorporation of the idea of what the West understood as "dependent sovereignty" in the treaty text.

Li Hongzhang had no choice but to put this issue aside during the negotiations in Tianjin, deciding to leave it for the signing in Korea instead. He meant to take steps to ensure that the United States acknowledged the tributary autonomy of Korea during the signing, even if it could not be specified in the treaty.

Part of Li's plan involved dispatching a Qing delegate to Korea to attend the treaty signing. His intention was to make sure that Korea and the United States understood each other, as well as to prevent any interference from Russia or Japan in the successful signing of the treaty. This delegate also had the mission of restoring the inclusion of the reference to Korea's tributary autonomy in the treaty if possible; or, if not, of devising an alternative plan to institute in its place.

The person who was sent to Korea to fulfill this task was Ma Jianzhong, who had also conducted clerical work in the negotiations with Shufeldt in Tianjin. He had his work cut out for him, as what lay in wait was the work of

U.S. Navy commodore Robert W. Shufeldt (1822–1895)
Photo courtesy of the Library of Congress

dealing with the discrepancy in the Qing's and Korea's understandings of tributary autonomy. Moreover, his task in hand naturally could not be separated from the movements of Japan, which was also engaged in treaty negotiations with Korea around this time. Ma Jianzhong would become aware of these issues firsthand on his arrival in Korea.

Ma Jianzhong arrived at Chemulp'o in Inch'ŏn, Korea, on May 8, 1882. In his presence, the treaty was signed without incident by Shufeldt and the Korean plenipotentiary Sin Hŏn on May 22. This U.S.-Korea treaty is referred to as the Shufeldt Treaty.

The reason for the two-week gap between Ma Jianzhong's arrival and the signing of the treaty was that various unexpected difficulties preceded the signing. For instance, despite departing at around the same time as Ma Jianzhong, bad weather delayed Shufeldt's arrival by as much as four days. In addition, during this two-week period, an incident of great significance occurred.

As perhaps might have been expected, Shufeldt did not change his mind about the inclusion of the proposed text on Korea's tributary autonomy for Article I of the treaty, and it thus failed to make it into the final treaty. Accordingly, a decision was made in which the Korean king would write an official letter to the American president, specifying the terms of Korea's tributary autonomy. In accordance with the terminology of the time, I will refer to this letter as an official communication from the Korean king (C. *zhaohui*).

Even after Shufeldt's arrival, it took time for Korea to coordinate the arrangements and prepare the paperwork. Indeed, it took until May 20 before everything from the official communication from the Korean king to the letter investing the Korean negotiators with plenipotentiary powers was ready. However, Ma Jianzhong brought forward the date that he included on the official communication from the Korean king, writing it as "May 15." This was a ploy designed to make it appear that the Americans had, in fact, acknowledged Korea's tributary autonomy during the treaty negotiations.

As Ma had predicted, Shufeldt objected to such a move. However, as this constituted a matter of pure paperwork, little furor erupted as a result of Ma's actions. What we should note, however, was that prior to Shufeldt's arrival, relations between Ma Jianzhong and the Koreans had turned sour, engendering new problems with regard to the Qing-Korea relationship.

The Role of Ma Jianzhong

Immediately upon Ma Jianzhong's arrival in Inch'ŏn, he asked the Korean officials who received him about the Korean government's intentions with regard to the treaty negotiations. They kept giving evasive answers, and even took a belittling attitude toward the Qing. This raised Ma's suspicions about the possibility of Japanese interference. This was because the Japanese minister in residence in Korea, Hanabusa Yoshimoto, had by chance reached Chemulp'o on the same day as Ma, and had already had occasion to meet with the Korean officials.

Ma then became livid, and began to intimidate the Korean officials. He gave the following account of events:

> Since having fallen prey to the seductions of the Japanese, while not going so far as to take an openly haughty and disrespectful attitude toward the Qing, the Koreans have nevertheless come to take a somewhat cunning tact toward us. On May 11, I vacated the accommodations prepared by the Koreans and returned to my ship, thereby hinting [to the Koreans] that a breakdown in relations had occurred. It was only then that they realized that they must not underestimate a Qing gentleman.

Here, we see that Ma determined that the insolence he faced from the Koreans was a product of their links to the Japanese. This gravely concerned him. The firm stance he took nevertheless seems to have paid off, as the Koreans adopted a much more submissive posture toward him after that. However, Ma was careful not to lower his guard:

On May 14, as a means of demonstrating our authority, when Sin Hŏn and Kim Hongjip, the chief and deputy delegates to the signing of the treaty, boarded my ship to pay their respects, in order to weaken the Koreans' spirit, I had them, in their king's stead, kneel three times and kowtow nine times, as well as reverently inquire about the well-being of the Empress Dowager and the Emperor. After having them do this, I then, in a calm and relaxed manner, proceeded to create an environment in which they would gladly listen to what it was I had to say. As I did this, I wrote out, on their behalf, a draft form of the official communication from the Korean king [for the American president]. While consenting to the use of the term "autonomy," [I also used this opportunity] to flesh out the reality of what constituted a "tributary." (*Dongxing chulu* [First Record of Ma Jianzhong's Journeys to Korea])

Here, Ma describes how, after having the Koreans perform the proper formalities associated with the Qing-Korean *zongshu* relationship, he entertained the Korean views on tariff rates and other matters, before finally exacting an agreement from them about how the official communication from the Korean king for the American president would be drawn up.

Ma Jianzhong summarized these acts as "giving them a taste of trembling with fear while keeping them still within my good graces." This was likely the old carrot-and-stick approach, which was also reflected in the significance Ma attached to the wording of the official communication from the Korean king. His conclusion was that, while the Qing should speak of Korea both in terms of its status as a "tributary" and in terms of its "autonomy," going forward, the Qing should take a more interventionist approach in Korea (treating it as what we might understand to be a "dependency" or "vassal state"), and that its "autonomy" ought to be made a nominal feature. Indeed, Ma thought that no aspect of Korean "autonomy" that contradicted Qing interests ought to be tolerated.

What Ma Jianzhong had faced on-site in Korea was the Japanese threat. Moreover, this was not the vague yet broad military threat that the Qing had felt for some years, but a more local, political

Qing diplomat Ma Jianzhong (1845–1900)

influence of Japan on Korea. This was because he saw the crafty and disrespectful attitude of the Korean officials as something that came from Japanese influence, or more specifically, the presence of Hanabusa Yoshimoto.

During his time in Korea, Ma reflected deeply on the bilateral relationship between Korea and the enemy threat that was Japan, and came to perceive that the relationship was infringing on the Qing's own relations with Korea. While Japan was an obvious threat, it was now also clear to him that the Qing could not blithely take Korean "submissiveness" for granted either. He thus had no choice but to try to eliminate this Japanese influence on Korea and strengthen Qing-Korean relations. It was for this reason that he came to attach a new meaning to the text about Korea's "tributary autonomy" found in the official communication from the Korean king destined for the American president.

The original aim of the official communication from the Korean king was to have the Western countries acknowledge Korea's "tributary autonomy," something that was not self-evident to them. Of course,

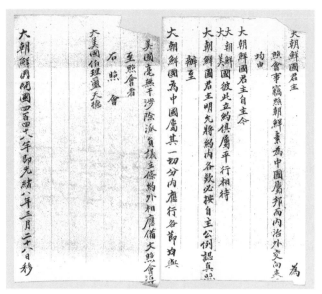

Facsimile of the official communication from the Korean king sent to the United States

Reproduced with permission from Okamoto Takashi, *Zokkoku to jishu no aida: Kindai Shin-Kan kankei to Higashi Ajia no meiun* [Between Dependency and Sovereignty: Modern Qing-Korean Relations and the Destiny of East Asia] (Nagoya: University of Nagoya Press, 2004).

from the Qing standpoint, the "tributary" aspect was of primary importance. Yet the Qing and Li Hongzhang had not had this clearly in mind from the outset. Nor had their thinking extended so far as to realize that definitions for the respective elements and relationship between "tributary" and "autonomy" were needed. However, in facing Korean insubordination in Korea—an attitude which was inconsistent with what was expected of a Qing "tributary"—Ma Jianzhong moved to endow the hitherto ambiguous and insufficiently defined concept of "tributary autonomy" with a clear meaning and direction.

The Imo Incident

Following Korea's conclusion of the Shufeldt Treaty, the country promptly concluded treaties with Britain and Germany, in succession. The terms were more or less the same as those of the Shufeldt Treaty, and the same official communication from the Korean king about "tributary autonomy" was, of course, appended. Ma Jianzhong was once again dispatched to Korea to attend the signings.

Having thus concluded treaties with Western countries, Korea had to be readied so that it could conform to those treaties as soon as they came into effect. While acting as an envoy to Korea, Ma Jianzhong was devising concrete measures to that end. However, before he put his plans into action, an unexpected incident came to pass. This was the Imo Incident.

The Imo Incident, triggered by a riot among ex-soldiers on July 23, 1882, did not simply end as a riot. Following attacks on the court and the killing of high officials, the Min regime collapsed, and the retired Taewŏn'gun Yi Haŭng came to wield actual power. Indeed, the events had effectively escalated into a full-blown coup d'état.

That was not all that transpired, however. The Japanese legation was also attacked, resulting in the murder of several Japanese as well as the threatening and banishment of Hanabusa Yoshimoto. This would serve to suddenly propel the incident into a serious diplomatic issue between Japan and Korea.

Despite having fled to Japan for dear life, Hanabusa was ordered back to Korea by the Japanese government, accompanied by four warships, three transport ships, and one army battalion. The government charged Hanabusa with a variety of tasks: to provide protection to Japanese nationals on Korean soil, to make the Korean government take responsibility for the riot, and to force the Koreans to agree to Japanese demands for several yet-to-be-settled trade regulations.

For the Qing, too, the Imo Incident became a major issue. It was not just an insurrection that had taken place within one of its tributaries. If matters continued as they did, Korea could be overwhelmed by Japanese military power and fall under Japanese influence. If that happened, the situation that the Qing had feared since the Japanese annexation of Ryukyu would become a reality. The sense of crisis that the Qing felt had encouraged the government to hurriedly dispatch Ma Jianzhong to Korea, with 3,000 soldiers in tow. The objective was to keep Japan in check and to subdue the insurrection. In this way, Japanese and Qing forces successively entered the Korean capital, creating a situation wherein one misstep could lead to war.

The Conclusion of the Imo Incident and
the Ensuing Japan-Qing Relationship

Hanabusa Yoshimoto reached Chemulp'o on August 12. He shook off Korean restraints and led his forces into the capital of Seoul on August 16. While the Taewŏn'gun regime gave him a friendly reception, they were not inclined to accept the Japanese demands.

Unhappy with the Korean stance, Hanabusa determined that this was "tantamount to a repudiation of negotiations" and gave what was in effect final notice before leaving the capital on August 23. The reason for the Taewŏn'gun's stance was that he trusted that the Qing would mediate, but the effect was nonetheless a sudden rise in tension.

Under such circumstances, Ma Jianzhong demonstrated remarkable skill. While Japan had already entered Seoul by the time he and his troops had arrived, Ma engaged in close contact with important persons in the Korean government as he attempted to form a clear view of the situation on the ground. As soon as negotiations between Hanabusa and the Taewŏn'gun had broken down, Ma took the opportunity to enter the capital once the Japanese had left. Ma then proceeded to abduct the Taewŏn'gun, whom he had already put off guard with his sweet talk, and sent him to China. This was on August 26.

In addition, Ma promptly proceeded to force the Korean government to return to the negotiation table with Japan. As this was happening, the Qing forces defeated the insurrectionist ex-soldiers and restored the Min regime to power. It was under such circumstances that the Chemulp'o Treaty and an additional convention to the Japan-Korea Treaty of Amity were concluded between Japan and Korea on August 30. These documents constituted a new turning point that would define the future of Japan-Korea relations thereafter.

Japan was, for the time being, satisfied with the conclusion of the

Chemulpŏ Treaty. In addition to having most of their demands accepted by the Koreans, such as those pertaining to the payment of reparations and the opening of Korean ports, this new treaty was the result of direct negotiations between Japan and Korea. Indeed, the Qing had not interfered in the negotiations as the Japanese had feared. In other words, Korea had negotiated "autonomously" with Japan as an "equal," just as had been stipulated in the Treaty of Kanghwa. However, that was just how things appeared on the surface.

Ma Jianzhong, who was in the Korean capital, did not simply observe the Japanese-Korean negotiations from a distance. He assumed quite the opposite stance, giving point-by-point instructions to the Korean plenipotentiary Kim Hongjip on how to respond to the Japanese demands. However, he was very careful to make sure that he avoided participation in the actual face-to-face negotiations. This outward appearance of Korean "autonomy" in its foreign relations, albeit nominal, was indispensable in order to get along with Japan, which saw Korea as an independent state, and to contain Japanese military power.

While Ma Jianzhong secured the agreement of the Korean king and important individuals for the abduction of the Taewŏn'gun and the subjugation of the ex-soldiers, he openly interfered with Korean internal politics, as was his plan from the beginning. Through these interventionist actions, he effectively treated Korea not as a traditional "tributary" but as a "dependency" or "vassal state."

This course of action that Ma Jianzhong took accorded with his own definition of "tributary autonomy," which effectively actualized Korea as a Qing "dependency" and nominalized its "autonomy." It might be more accurate to say that Ma Jianzhong's way of thinking led him naturally to act as he did. That being the case, this new interventionist policy would not draw to a close with the settlement of the Imo Incident.

Remedial Measures and "Tributary Autonomy"

Before the Imo Incident, Ma Jianzhong had made use of his experience as a two-time envoy to Korea to formulate his own concrete Korea

Cho Yŏngha (1845–1884), Korean thanksgiving and notification envoy

policy. The Imo Incident happened just as he was about to present his policy to both the Korean king and his superior Li Hongzhang, putting an abrupt stop to his plans and forcing him to go to Korea. Thus, from Ma Jianzhong's standpoint, the settlement of the Imo Incident meant that he could resume these activities.

On September 7, 1882, Ma Jianzhong arrived back in Tianjin, accompanied by Thanksgiving and Notification Envoy Cho Yŏngha and Deputy Envoy Kim Hongjip, who had been dispatched to Tianjin by the Korean government. Both had been involved in the signing of the treaties with the Western countries and had also worked closely with Ma during the Imo Incident, and they were thus on good terms with him. In particular, Cho Yŏngha was from a noted family and was the nephew of Shinjŏngwanghu (Queen Sinjong), the formal regent during King Kojong's minority.

On the face of it, their mission was officially to go to Beijing and "give thanks" to the Qing emperor for suppressing the Imo Incident, as well as to "notify" him of the Taewŏngun's homecoming. Yet their actual objective was to meet with Li Hongzhang in Tianjin to discuss the future of Korean foreign relations and Qing-Korean relations after the opening of the Korean ports.

Cho Yŏngha repeatedly met with Li Hongzhang, Ma Jianzhong, and their subordinates between early September and the end of November 1882. As a result, they decided on the furnishing of a loan to Korea, the setting up of a customs service, and a program for mining development. They also hired the foreign consultant Paul G. von Möllendorff and a number of Chinese staff to assist with these projects. All returned to Korea on December 3.

While it was said that Cho Yŏngha was the one who brought up these matters for discussion, it was Ma Jianzhong who actually proposed them. Ma probably had the Koreans suggest plans that he himself had come up with as a way to make it seem like the plans had originated from their autonomous ideas while he was actually attempting to make Korea act according to the Qing's wishes. This was another aspect of the nominalization of Korean "autonomy."

The loan and the program for mine development were handled by the China Merchants Steam Navigation Company, a modern company under Li Hongzhang's control, while Möllendorff, who had been recommended by Li Hongzhang and Ma Jianzhong, set up the Korean Maritime Customs Service. Ma Jianchang, elder brother of Ma Jianzhong, served as a consultant to the Korean king in his younger brother's stead, as the younger Ma was too busy to remain in Korea himself.

In terms of outcomes, none of these measures accomplished anything other than a strengthening of Korea's dependence on the Qing, thereby very much actualizing the former's status as a Qing "dependency." Ma Jianzhong had worked hard to ensure that these decisions had been made in the form of Korean "autonomy," when they were in fact his own proposals and were actualizing Korea's "dependency" status.

The underlying motivation for these efforts was, of course, Japan. The right to develop Korea's mines was a concession that Japan had originally sought to obtain, and the loan from the Qing government was similarly devised to counteract the reparations Korea had been forced to pay Japan after the signing of the Chemulp'o Treaty. The collateral for that loan was the customs revenue from the newly established Korean Maritime Customs Service. Thus, the loan, the customs service, and the program of mine development constituted a three-part plan that served to counteract Japanese machinations in Korea. This was Ma Jianzhong's response to the collusion between the fear-instilling Japanese and the Koreans that he had encountered on the occasion of the signing of the Shufeldt Treaty.

"Tributary Autonomy" and Korean Dependency

Of course, these plans were just the beginning for the new Qing role in Korean affairs. This situation was expressed more explicitly in the text of the Regulations for Maritime and Overland Trade between Chinese and Korean Subjects, concluded around the same time.

This text was a commercial treaty that permitted maritime trade between the Qing and Korea, and stipulated the stationing of commercial representatives (i.e., consuls) in both countries. However, it was nothing short of an unequal treaty that favored Qing interests over that of the Koreans. Despite its unequal treaty-like character, the text itself was deliberately referred to not as a "treaty" but as a set of "regulations." This was to emphasize that the agreement constituted an agreement on an administrative matter between a suzerain (i.e., the Qing) and its dependency, or vassal state (i.e., Korea). However, while the relationship between the two parties had changed, with the Qing taking a more interventionist role in Korean affairs, it is important to bear in mind that Korea was still referred to as a "tributary." Indeed, the preamble of the treaty, too, expressly declared that "Korea is a Qing tributary."

Here, too, it was Ma Jianzhong who led the negotiations, about which he wrote the following:

The trade regulations decided on now are essentially different from a treaty concluded by equal countries. If it is truly feared that other nations will make demands with reference to these regulations, then the following passage can be included at the end or the beginning:

"Korea has long been a tributary of China, and the regulations for maritime and overland trade determined here are meant to give preferential treatment to a tributary of China. Hence, these regulations are not a precedent for the equality of friendly nations."

If Korea's desire is to make these regulations the same as treaties with other countries, that means simply that Korea secretly wants to be an equal of the Qing, that Korea fears only the Japanese, and that Korea does not fear the Qing. (*Qingji Zhong-Ri-Han guanxi shiliao* [Sources on Sino-Japanese-Korean Relations in the Late Qing Era])

It is clear that the aim was to increase Korea's dependence on the Qing, and that the motivating factor for these changes to the Qing-Korean relationship was Japan.

In this way, Korea began to open up the country and its ports to outside influence toward the end of 1882. Within the context of their treaties with the Western powers and Japan, the restored Min regime also moved to embark on a new set of modernization policies. By this time, the howls of those who wanted to defend the neo-Confucian orthodoxy and reject the heterodoxy of Western thought had long since died down, and the *Ch'ŏkhwabi* had come to be dismantled on a country-wide basis. Unconditionally rejecting the West and xenophobically viewing it as an enemy became a thing of the past, at least on a governmental level.

Yet amid all of this was the Qing, seeking to champion the principle of "tributary autonomy" for Korea. Even after the conclusion of the Imo Incident, the Qing maintained a military presence in the country, stationing 3,000 soldiers in Seoul. Furthermore, it also took a variety of measures that were aimed at increasing Korean dependency on the Qing. Such measures were naturally implicated in Korea's modernization policies as well.

Both Japan—the prime motivation for this new form of Qing involvement in Korea—and the Western powers could not suppress their misgivings about this new reconfiguration of the Qing-Korean relationship, which was championed by the Qing as "tributary autonomy." What is more, Korea, too, was far from satisfied with the Qing's new approach to its "tributary autonomy." As it would transpire, these misgivings, and the actions they came to motivate, would come to greatly shape the future course of East Asian history.

CHAPTER THREE

The Development of "Tributary Autonomy"

1. Korea's Pursuit of "Autonomy"

The Treaties with the West

King Kojong of Korea dispatched Pak Yŏnghyo, the son-in-law of the former King Ch'ŏljong, to Japan as friendship ambassador on September 7, 1882. This was the same day that Ma Jianzhong and the Cho Yŏngha delegation arrived in Tianjin. This envoy was tasked with delivering an apology to Japan in accordance with Article VI of the Chemulp'o Treaty, and with exchanging the ratified copies of the additional convention to the Japan-Korea Treaty of Amity. The delegation also included the advisor Kim Okkyun, who had been to Japan before, and an attendant, Min Yŏngik, a nephew of the queen. They left Korea with Hanabusa Yoshimoto on September 21 and arrived in Tokyo on October 13.

The mission tasked to the Pak Yŏnghyo delegation went beyond the execution of official business with Japan. Indeed, they had another mission to perform, for which they had most likely been briefed by King Kojong himself: to request the approval and ratification of the other treaties Korea had signed with the United States, Britain, and Germany from the various foreign ministers who were stationed in Japan.

Korea's treaties with these countries had all been signed prior to the Imo Incident. However, the outbreak of such an unforeseen crisis may well have catalyzed these foreign powers to doubt Korea's commitment to engage diplomatically with them. As such, the task of the Pak Yŏnghyo delegation was to convey that the Korean government remained committed to the treaties and to ask that the signatories acknowledge the same.

If the Pak Yŏnghyo delegation was only going to convey these messages in a purely administrative manner to the foreign ministers stationed in Japan, there would be little need for us to evaluate this episode here. This is because Cho Yŏngha and his party conveyed messages of a similar ilk to their diplomatic counterparts in Beijing. However, the Pak delegation to Japan is an important episode as the delegation, in addition to conveying a similar set of messages to the Cho delegation, made its own unique set of statements to members of the Japan-based *corps diplomatique*.

Pak Yŏnghyo (1861–1939), Korean friendship delegate to Japan and chief envoy Reproduced with permission from *Shashin de shiru Kankoku no dokuritsu undō* [The Korean Independence Movement in Photographs], pt. 1 (Tokyo: Kokusho Kankōkai, 1988).

These exchanges were written down in detail by the British minister to Japan, Harry S. Parkes. The following excerpts are taken from his report to the British Foreign Office.

First, there was a statement by Min Yŏngik. He made the following remarks with regard to Ma Jianzhong's kidnapping of the Taewŏn'gun:

The removal of the Taewŏn'gun was not a bad thing for Korea, but the manner in which it was conducted constitutes a kind of national humiliation. The Qing does not have the right to interfere with Korean domestic politics in such a manner.

According to Parkes, Min went on to emphasize that it was stipulated in the official communication from the Korean king that "the management of its government affairs, domestic and foreign, has always been vested in the sovereign," pointing out

That the tributary reletion [*sic*] of Corea to China were confined to

certain ceremonial observances, and that China never had interfered with the internal administration of Corea. Her recent action
was therefore quite opposed to previous practice.

Min concluded his remarks by stating that "the Korean people cannot
bear this interference by the Qing."
Next, Pak Yŏnghyo, the chief envoy, said the following:

We have no military forces as they are not needed to govern our
people, and thus, it is Korea's current predicament that we are in the
hands of the Qing, cannot resist them and must do as they say. The
official communication sent by the Korean king to the heads of state
of the Western countries with whom we have concluded treaties
declare that, while Korea is indeed a tributary of the Qing, it enjoys
autonomy in its domestic politics and foreign affairs. This declaration of the king's independent position is fully approved by the
Qing as well. Regardless, the Qing are now trying to interfere with
Korean domestic politics and foreign affairs in every way they can,
seeking to deprive the king of his sovereignty and the government
of its freedom to act.

The above statements reveal that both Min and Pak shared a similar
stance toward Korea's status vis-à-vis the Qing: namely, that Korea was
undoubtedly "independent" and ought not constitute a subservient
power to the Qing dynasty. This therefore meant that all action taken
by the Qing in the wake of the Imo Incident constituted a reprehensible form of "interference" for them both. However, at the same time,
we must also bear in mind that Min and Pak made these statements to
the Japan-based diplomatic community in the capacity of representatives of the Korean government. The ideas and ideals that they articulated ought therefore to be understood as giving a voice to a larger
contingent of the Korean people.
Pak Yŏnghyo, Min Yŏngik, and Kim Okkyun were of the same

opinion, and to them, Korea's "independent position" was guaranteed by the official communication from the Korean king. Despite this, it was clear to them that Korea was, at the time, being subjected to unjust interference due to its lack of military power. Forging direct relationships with the Western powers as quickly as possible thus constituted a task of utmost importance. Doing so would mean that these countries would have to acknowledge and respect Korean autonomy, and would therefore allow for a rectification of the present inequity that Korea faced. Such was the

Min Yŏngik (1860–1914), a nephew of the Korean queen

Reproduced with permission from Tabohashi Kiyoshi, *Kindai Nis-Sen kankei no kenkyū* [Research on Early Modern Japanese-Korean Relations], pt. 1 (Tokyo: Hara Shobō, 1973).

hope and vision that Pak, Min, and Kim held for Korea's future.

The Koreans would not have to wait long. The United States soon ratified the Shufeldt Treaty, thereby acceding to the Koreans' request. While Britain and Germany, in their own treaties with Korea, had some qualms about conditions relating to such matters as tariff rates and thus decided against ratification, they nevertheless chose to conclude new treaties with Korea in 1883. Furthermore, Russia, too, came to sign a treaty with Korea in the following year.

Of the three treaties that Korea had signed with Britain, Germany, and Russia, none had seen Qing intervention. Instead, they had all been concluded following direct negotiations between the Korean government and these countries' plenipotentiaries in Seoul, the Korean capital. This likely gave the Koreans reason to believe that they had finally managed, as had been described in the various official communication from the Korean king, to exercise their "autonomy in foreign affairs," and had thereby solidified their "independent position" in international society.

The Road Leading Up to the Kapsin Coup

Such a sanguine outlook did not mean that Qing pressure on Korea had abated, however. In the first place, the Qing had understood the official communication from the Korean king that articulated Korea's "tributary autonomy" as proof that their relationship had evolved into one in which the Qing could take greater control in Korean affairs. Indeed, those actions on the part of the Qing that Pak Yŏnghyo and Kim Okkyun had considered as a form of reprehensible "interference" were simply a matter of the Qing exercising what they perceived to be their given rights.

In this sense, then, given the divergence in perceptions, it would be unreasonable to expect the Qing to have been more considerate toward the perspective and conduct of the Korean side. And, from the Qing perspective at the very least, there was no need to actively pursue a course of non-interference.

This attitude on the part of the Qing therefore compelled Korea to take a clearer approach to what it was that it wanted to achieve. Expelling foreigners was no longer an option, and the country had become irreversibly set upon a course of opening up. However, such developments did not necessarily indicate a total victory of the so-called Korean "Enlightenment Faction." In advancing Korea down such a path, members of the faction were forced to decide between abiding by the Qing's policy directives or protesting them. Eventually, this led to an internal schism, revealing a clear antagonism and split between moderates and radicals: the former were the so-called Serving-the-Great Party, and the latter the so-called Independence Party.

Interestingly, this divide was evident in the Korean delegations dispatched to China and Japan in the wake of the Imo Incident. The Cho Yŏngha delegation to China was of a moderate bent. Meanwhile, the Pak Yŏnghyo and Kim Okkyun delegation to Japan firmly sat in the radical camp. It is unclear whether such an outcome was either a product of the particular tasks and roles delegated to them, or whether their pre-existing ambitions and political leanings resulted in the delegation of these particular tasks. Perhaps both aspects played a part.

One way of understanding the allegiances and political beliefs to which these two parties subscribed is to position them (a) as individually inheriting, or supporting, one facet of Korea's traditional pre-eighteenth century relationships, and (b) in conjunction with what was implied by either the term "tributary" or "autonomy," as found in the official communication from the Korean king and the treaties Korea signed in the late nineteenth century. The Serving-the-Great Party comprised, in effect, ideological inheritors and advocates of the Qing-Korean *zongshu* relationship, and supported Korea's subsistence as a Qing "tributary." Meanwhile, the Independence Party can be understood as the ideological inheritors of the "neighborly" relationship between Korea and Japan, and were advocates of full-blown "autonomy" or independence for Korea.

Kim Okkyun (1851–1894), member of the Korean delegation to Japan
Reproduced with permission from *Shashin de shiru Kankoku no dokuritsu undō* [The Korean Independence Movement in Photographs], pt. 1 (Tokyo: Kokusho Kankōkai, 1988).

Seen from the perspective of the factional rivalries that were playing out at the time, the Serving-the-Great Party constituted the dominant force, as it counted many important people from the Min administration among its ranks. Meanwhile, the Independence Party occupied a decidedly minor position. This was because none of the activities it had planned had borne fruit, whether attempts at institutional reform or attempts at loan procurement.

For the Independence Party, while Qing pressure was an obvious factor, the root cause of its successive failings came down to none other than the rival Serving-the-Great Party, which aided, abetted, and embraced this Qing pressure. Such actions rapidly intensified the antagonism between the two parties, eventually leading to Kim Okkyun, together with Pak Yŏnghyo and other like-minded individuals, to plot and, on December 4, 1884, execute a coup d'état. This is known as the Kapsin Coup.

Korea's International Position

Having killed or wounded key people in government and taken control of the royal palace, the Independence Party seized control of political power with the temporary support of King Kojong. However, three days after the outbreak of the coup, 1,500 Qing soldiers under the command of Yuan Shikai intervened in the crisis, bringing a swift end to the new government. Kim Okkyun and Pak Yŏnghyo fled to Japan.

From the outset, this coup d'état, which had failed after just three days, was not a political struggle waged on a purely domestic basis. Rather, it was an international issue that involved both the Qing and Japan as well. In the first place, its execution had been backed by support from the Japanese legation, and Qing troops had brought the coup to a close by launching an attack on that same legation. Moreover, as apparent in the events of the crisis, it also served as a reflection of the country's wavering international allegiances.

As evinced by the split between the Serving-the-Great Party and the Independence Party, there was a divergence of views in Korea as to how the country should approach its foreign relations. For example, the cases of Cho Yŏngha and Pak Yŏnghyo, who were both close to the royal family and stood at opposite ends of the abovementioned political divide, reveal how individual circumstances and political views could drive people apart.

However, these divisions were not always so clear cut. Min Yŏngik, the rising star of the Min clan who had accompanied Pak Yŏnghyo and Kim Okkyun to Japan, had initially been critical of the Qing and was a strong advocate of Korean "independence." Yet, after being sent to the United States the following year, he developed a taste for leadership in the serving-the-great camp. In this way, an individual could oscillate between the two extremes. Indeed, it was highly unlikely that the political views of Min Yŏngik could have just transformed overnight.

That being the case, we should not consider the two poles as entirely separate, but rather as variations that were tied to a common ideological axis. The terms "moderates" and "radicals" likewise help to express this subtle distinction. However, it was not just attitudes toward Korea's "modernization" that oscillated relative to a shared central ideological axis or reference point. Indeed, the same was true of attitudes toward how Korea should engage with the outside world. And,

Ŏ Yunjung (1848–1896), member of the Serving-the-Great Party

Reproduced with permission from Tabohashi Kiyoshi, *Kindai Nis-Sen kankei no kenkyū* [Research on Early Modern Japanese-Korean Relations], pt. 2 (Tokyo: Hara Shobō, 1973).

in this case, it was the statement found in Korea's official communication from the Korean king that "Corea is a dependency of China, although 'the management of its government affairs, domestic and foreign, has always been vested in the sovereign,'" that served as that common axis or reference point.

With this in mind, I would now like to introduce the following statement by Ŏ Yunjung, who was both a moderate and a member of the Serving-the-Great Party:

It is fine to say that Korea has autonomy, but it is wrong to call ourselves independent. Since the rise of the Qing, we have rightly submitted to tributary relations with them. How can we then call ourselves independent? (*Qingji Zhong-Ri-Han guanxi shiliao* [Sources of Sino-Japanese-Korean Relations in the Late Qing Era])

We should note that this statement, which refutes the Japanese claim of Korean "independence," nonetheless accepts the notion of Korean "autonomy," and referred to the relationship with the Qing in the ceremonial sense of "submitting to tributary relations with [the Qing]."

Meanwhile, radical Independence Party member Yun Ch'iho had this to say on the matter:

> We immediately became an independent country on the day we concluded treaties with the United States, Britain, and the other powers. This is because there is no principle in this world that dictates that an equal treaty can be concluded with a vassal state (K. *sokkuk*, C. *shuguo*). (*Yun Ch'iho ilgi* [Diary of Yun Ch'iho])

For Yun, "autonomy" meant "independence." What is more, he parses the concept of a *sokkuk* or *shuguo* not in its traditional sense as a "tributary," but as how "the world," which very much includes us today, understands the term to mean a "vassal state" or "dependency." He then went on to deliberately attempt to deny the validity of Korea's status as a "vassal."

Looking at both arguments, they share the understanding that Korea is "autonomous" but differ in how they view the concept of a *sokkuk* or *shuguo* as either constituting a "tributary" or a "vassal state." In other words, the variations in their respective views were determined by the respective stances they took toward the Qing.

Searching for a Solution around the Time of the Coup

While the official communication from the Korean king claimed that Korea was a "tributary" of the Qing, as Pak Yŏngik explained to Parkes, the specific content implied by the use of the term was simply that the country was obligated to partake in "certain forms of ceremonial," such as the offering of tribute, and did not directly imply that Korea was dependent upon the Qing. Such was the common understanding among all Koreans.

Even so, the Qing used this tributary status as a pretext to apply pressure on Korea. That being the case, the question then became, should one accept that pressure as inevitable to some extent, or should one reject it completely? Kim Okkyun and the other instigators of the coup took the latter position.

On December 5, 1884, the day after the coup was launched, Kim and his peers established a new government and issued a declaration that the country would undergo a program of reform. The first provision thereof, which was appended to a demand for the Taewŏn'gun's return to Korea, stated that Korea will "debate and abolish the empty ritual of paying tribute [to the Chinese emperor]."

Yun Ch'iho (1865–1945), member of the radical Independence Party
Reproduced with permission from *Yun Ch'iho* (Seoul: Korean History Compilation Committee, 1927–1935).

Indeed, bringing an end to Qing pressure required that Korea first repudiate the pretexts that enabled such interference in the first place: namely, Korea's tributary status and the "empty ritual of paying tribute" itself. The declaration itself was likely a product of Korea's drawing such a conclusion.

Of course, were Korea to adopt this approach, it would mean confronting the Qing head-on. Unsurprisingly then, a conflict with the Qing did indeed occur, but Kim and his peers' direct and radical approach was mercilessly stamped out. Excessive radicalism hit the wall of reality and was proven impracticable.

That being said, from the Korean perspective, so long as the country exercised "autonomy," it was by no means obligated to unconditionally yield to Qing pressure. What is more, a policy of obsequious cooperation with the Qing authorities who had come to be stationed in Korea was, for the Korean government, particularly morally reprehensible.

The reasons for this were clear: After the Kapsin Coup, Li Hongzhang had taken a much more blatant stance in his efforts to contain the Korean government. On top of stationing the young and energetic Yuan Shikai in Korea as Qing representative, he also returned the Taewŏn'gun, who had been held in China, to the country.

With the help of Qing troops, the Min regime was once again restored to power. However, despite being offered this lifeline by the Qing, the Min could not help but harbor a sense of enmity and distrust toward the Qing, who had protected their bitter enemy, the Taewŏn'gun. The Min also sought to distance themselves from moderates Kim Yunsik and Kim Hongjip at this time, perceiving them as being too close to the Qing. And, it was under such circumstances that the Korean government began to explore a new policy of "autonomy" that was neither explicitly anti- nor pro-Qing.

Subsequently, however, relations with the Qing deteriorated and crises flared up almost annually. In 1886, for instance, the Qing suspected that Korea had entered into a secret agreement with Russia that would entitle the country to Russian protection. Furthermore, in 1887, a dispute broke out between Korea and the Qing when Korea moved to dispatch its first permanent ministers—invested with full plenipotentiary powers—to the United States and Europe without first consulting the Qing. And, in 1888, Korea concluded an overland trade treaty directly with Russia, raising further suspicions about the existence of a secret treaty between the two countries.

A third party, however, was also highly implicated in these growing antagonisms between Korea and the Qing: the foreign advisors of the Korean government. Indeed, these men were involved in practically all of these incidents, playing an exceedingly prominent role in each. Furthermore, it would be no exaggeration to claim that the views of the Korean government at the time found full articulation in the words and actions of these foreigners.

The Appointment of Owen N. Denny

The two most noted foreign advisors of the Korean government in the 1880s were Paul G. von Möllendorff and Owen N. Denny. The former being a German linguist, and the latter an American lawyer, they had nothing obvious in common. However, their careers had many similarities: both had served as diplomats for their respective countries in China and were extremely close to Li Hongzhang.

As discussed above, these foreign advisors were dispatched following the Imo Incident on the suggestion of the Qing, or, more precisely, of Ma Jianzhong. As such, both the initially appointed Möllendorff and his successor Denny were intended to be Qing mouthpieces under the sponsorship of Li Hongzhang.

Yet the reality was very different. The Qing-Korean relations of the time operated in such a way as to lead the two to stand in stark opposition to the Qing.

While I will discuss Möllendorff's case later, it was Denny, serving the Korean government from 1886 to 1890, who came to give written articulation to the assertions and stance of Korea at the time.

Denny was born in Ohio, but came to call Oregon home after moving there as a boy. After serving as a judge in the state, he went to China to serve as a consul in the American consular service. He was promoted all the way from consul in Tianjin to consul general in Shanghai. It was during these years of consular service that he became closely acquainted with Li Hongzhang.

Denny left China in late 1883 to return to the United States. In July 1885, at his home in Portland, he received a telegram from China inviting him back to Tianjin. He accepted and left the United States toward the end of that same year. After meeting and engaging in discussions with Li Hongzhang in Tianjin, he took up his new position in the Korean capital at the end of March 1886.

Li Hongzhang had great expectations for Denny's legal expertise. In particular, Li wanted to make use of Denny's knowledge about international law, on which the Western countries relied, to preemptively

Owen N. Denny (1838–1900), American lawyer and advisor to Korea
Photo courtesy of the Oregon Historical Society Library

keep those countries that had misgivings about the relationship between the Qing and Korea from upsetting the status quo in Korea. Denny was paired with Yuan Shikai, who had been stationed earlier as Qing resident in Korea, and the two were tasked with guiding the Korean government in the direction desired by the Qing.

However, the issue of whether what Li Hongzhang had envisioned for the mission tallied with the perceptions of others was an entirely separate matter. This was true not only for both the Western powers and the Korean government but also for Denny himself.

Shortly after taking up his position in Korea, Denny discovered that Yuan Shikai was exceedingly high-handed in his treatment of the country. Yuan not only interfered in the domestic politics and foreign affairs of Korea at every turn but also tolerated and even encouraged Chinese people to engage in smuggling and other illegal acts in the country. What is more, Yuan went so far as to threaten the king and his position. These were all outrageous acts in Denny's eyes.

Denny repeatedly called for Yuan's dismissal, and even tried speaking to Li Hongzhang directly. He was convinced that it was his duty to try and bring a stop to Yuan Shikai's tyranny.

Denny's Pamphlet: *China and Korea*

Around the time of the conclusion of his two-year service, which had been marked by all-out antagonism with Yuan Shikai, Denny determined to publish a text that criticized Qing policy on Korea. The result was a pamphlet titled *China and Korea* (1888).

As *China and Korea* was issued as a pamphlet, one can understand it as being designed more or less as a propaganda tool drawn up with a very specific purpose in mind. The assertions it voiced, too, were very much those of Denny and Denny alone. However, at the same time, the content Denny gave voice to did not so much express his personal views as much as it did the international position desired by the Koreans themselves. As such, it deserves a close reading. Let us look at one important passage:

International law will keep an account of their development too, and in its vigilance for the rights of the weak, will keep an account of Korea also in her struggle for the maintenance of independent state-hood. After having been by the great nations of the international world literally dragged from that seclusion which had for so many centuries enveloped the little kingdom in mystery, to join the family of civilized nations under the expressed guarantee of assistance in the event of oppression or unjust treatment, those powers will surely not permit the stultification of this assurance by allowing their younger member to be strangled at the very threshold of its international life.

This passage argued that Korea's treaties with Western countries implied international recognition of Korean "independence," which meant that Korea's efforts to realize its "independence" were justified under international law. Therefore, obstructing that "independence" was internationally impermissible. This agrees with the views expressed by Yun Ch'iho, as seen earlier.

Then again, Denny did not *just* emphasize Korean "independence":

Korea, however, is a tributary state of China; relations have been sustained in the past with the utmost good faith, and which Korea desires in all sincerity to continue so long as China's treatment is generous, friendly and just. But the tributary relations one state

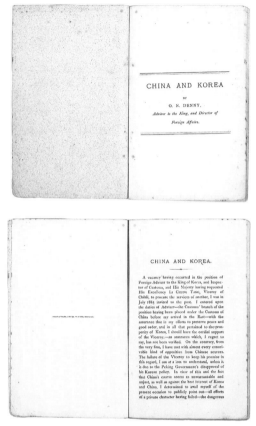

China and Korea, a pamphlet by O. N. Denny
Reproduced with permission from O. N. Denny, *Shin-Kan ron* [China and Korea], trans. and ed. by Okamoto Takashi (Tokyo: Seibunsha, 2010).

may hold to another do not and cannot in any degree affect its sovereign and independent rights. For this reason, the tribute annually paid by Korea to China does not impair Korean sovereignty or independence. (*China and Korea*)

Here we see that Denny not only acknowledged the existence of tributary relations between the Qing and Korea, but even stated that Korea wanted to continue that "traditional relationship." This was precisely what, as we saw above, Ŏ Yunjung emphasized. This passage reveals that Denny, too, did not intend to deny this facet of the Qing-Korea relationship.

However, the acceptance of such a premise for Qing-Korean relations did not constitute a hindrance to Korean "independence" under international law. Citing Henry Wheaton's 1836 *Elements of International Law* to substantiate this argument, Denny asserted that Korea's attitude and actions fully complied with international law. He also denied that the strange state of Qing-Korean relations at the time was Korea's responsibility, instead blaming it on "the illegal and high-handed treatment Korea is now receiving at the hands of the Chinese, and their studied and persistent attempts to destroy Korean sovereignty by absorbing the country."

Denny's Reasoning

The excerpts we saw above help to give a clear sense of the central argument that runs through *China and Korea*. With this in mind, let us now move on to examine how this argument relates to the issue of Korea's "tributary autonomy."

China and Korea's central thesis was much contingent upon the content found in the Korean king's official communication to the American president. For that reason, the pamphlet's stance was in complete agreement with the position of the Korean government. This should not come as a surprise. In writing the pamphlet, Denny himself was attempting both to give a voice to the stance and opinions that Korea held at that time, and to make them clearer.

As an American, and a native speaker of English, Denny naturally relied upon the English version of the Korean king's official communication to make his case. His internal thought process, too, was inevitably conducted through the medium of English. The English version of the official communication renders the term *sokkuk* or *shuguo* (i.e., "tributary") in English as "a state tributary to China," while the term for *chaju* or *zizhu* (i.e., "autonomy") was rendered as "full sovereignty."

Using these translations of these technical terms as a basis, Denny cited international law in his pamphlet to derive a schema that equated a tributary country to an independent one.

This therefore meant that if the term "tributary" in the Chinese-language version of the official communication was, say, rendered as "vassal state" in English, and that if the power dynamic inherent in a suzerain-vassal relationship was subsequently applied to the Qing's relationship with Korea, this would constitute not only a gross misunderstanding, but also an illicit act as well. After all, an independent state could not simultaneously function as a vassal state. However, understood from another angle, this also meant that so long as the two countries continued to interact according to the terms of tribute relations, and continued to embrace the other ceremonial aspects of their bilateral relationship, no disagreement over what was meant by the concept of "tributary" in the Korean king's official communication ought to emerge.

Following the Imo Incident, an extreme diversity in opinion on how to understand and approach the concepts of "tributary" and "autonomy" could be witnessed in the Korean political world, as evinced by the separation and antagonism between the Serving-the-Great and Independence parties. Any unifying sense of direction for the "autonomy" concept was utterly shattered by the Kapsin Coup, and the "tributary" concept met a similar fate after the Taewŏn'gun's return to Korea.

That being so, it stands to reason that the surviving regime possessed its own definition of "tributary autonomy." And with the publication of Denny's *China and Korea*, that definition was thrown into sharp relief. Indeed, for the regime, to be a "tributary" was to engage in nothing more than the ceremonial procedure of tribute, while the nature of "autonomy" corresponded with the notion of "independence" as found in international law. Korea's intention at the time was to deviate from neither of these definitions.

The primary purpose of writing *China and Korea* in English was to make an appeal to a foreign audience about the Korean predicament. However, as Denny anticipated the publication of a Chinese version as well, it was evident that it was also designed to act as a critique of Qing policy on Korea. The Qing and Li Hongzhang were quick to realize this, expressing their deep displeasure with Denny and the content of *China and Korea*. Furthermore, they also directed their anger toward the Korean government for unilaterally extending Denny's employment contract. From the Qing perspective, while Denny himself constituted a problem, the bigger issue at hand was the attitude of the Koreans who had protected him and let him do as he pleased.

Denny's actions had, after all, been diametrically opposed to Li Hongzhang's initial aim: to send him to Korea to do the Qing's bidding. Despite this, as soon as Denny arrived in Korea, he came into conflict with Yuan Shikai, the Qing resident in Korea, and went as far as to publish the *China and Korea* pamphlet. This was an extremely ironic twist for Li Hongzhang, and we have to conclude that there was a difference in perceptions between the two from the outset.

Moreover, this divergence in perceptions on the role of the Qing in Korea was not limited merely to Li Hongzhang and Denny. It also existed at the intergovernmental level between the Qing and Korea.

While the *China and Korea* pamphlet succeeded in bringing further clarity to the Korean position at the time, what position did the Qing take? In order to consider this question, we have to delve further back in time.

2. The Qing's Pursuit of a "Tributary"

The Qing and the Kapsin Coup

Indeed, no sooner had the Qing begun to institute such a policy than it faced multiple setbacks in the form of covert resistance from Korea and from the other foreign powers. One key setback was the return to China, after less than a year in Korea, of Ma Jianzhong's elder brother Ma Jianchang, who had been sent to the country as Jianzhong's substitute. Another was the direct conclusion of new treaties with Korea by Britain and Germany.

Yet, despite such setbacks, the Qing's new policy prescriptions for Korea did, for the most part, manage to endure, until the Kapsin Coup erupted. The Qing's troops had remained stationed in the Korean capital, and it had enjoyed the support of a pro-Qing government. However, the the Kapsin Coup and the slew of events that occurred in its wake upended this status quo.

Although the Kapsin Coup ended in failure, this did not mean that the Qing would see a return to the status quo ante. Indeed, although the pro-Japanese faction of the Korean government collapsed, the pro-Qing faction ousted in the coup did not return to power. Above all, the subsequent developments on the Korean side came to pose an even greater threat to the Qing's influence upon the country.

The determining factor for Qing policy in Korea had been the threat posed by Japan. If Korea were annexed by Japan as the Ryukyu islands had been, that would pose a serious threat to Qing security. As we saw above, the Qing had influenced Korea to conclude treaties with Western powers and had sought to make the underlying principles of Korea's "tributary autonomy" explicit. All of these measures had been taken as a result of the threat posed by Japan.

The decline in Japanese influence in Korea after the Kapsin Coup likely served as a great encouragement to the Qing. Indeed, it really seemed that things were going their way. However, before long, Korea made a move that would take the Qing greatly by surprise: it chose to ally with Russia. At the forefront of this new political gambit stood the foreign advisor Paul G. von Möllendorff.

Möllendorff and the Secret Agreement between Russia and Korea

Möllendorff was born in the town of Zehdenick, north of Berlin. After engaging in study in the fields of Oriental studies and linguistics at the University of Halle, in 1869, he went to China, where he was employed by the Chinese Imperial Maritime Customs Service, an organization managed by Westerners. In 1874, he became a diplomat in the service of the German Empire, eventually rising to the position of vice-consul in Tianjin. In this post, he would become closely acquainted with both Li Hongzhang and Ma Jianzhong. In 1881, he resigned his vice-consulship due to a deterioration in relations with Max von Brandt, the then German minister in Beijing. However, in July of the following year, his career would take a new turn when he was approached by the Qing about the possibility of serving in Korea. The series of events that led up to this arrival in Seoul are as described earlier in this chapter.

After arriving in Seoul, Möllendorff took control of the country's trade affairs and diplomatic negotiations, simultaneously discharging the functions of inspector general of the Korean Maritime Customs Service and foreign vice-minister. He also took charge of a number of related economic and educational initiatives, working most diligently.

During his tenure in the Korean government, he clashed with Kim Okkyun over issues pertaining to the minting of the new Korean currency and the use of customs revenues, thereby becoming an irreconcilable

Paul G. von Möllendorff (1847–1901), German linguist and advisor to Korea
Reproduced with permission from Tabohashi Kiyoshi, *Kindai Nis-Sen kankei no kenkyū* [Research on Early Modern Japanese-Korean Relations], pt. 2 (Tokyo: Hara Shobō, 1973).

political enemy of the Independence Party. For this reason, he actively sought to suppress Kim Okkyun and his associates during the Kapsin Coup.

However, the fact that Möllendorff sought to suppress the pro-Japanese Independence Party did not therefore mean that he took a particularly pro-Qing stance. Despite Möllendorff viewing Kim Okkyun as a political enemy, he nevertheless agreed with Kim that the pressure the Qing had been applying to Korea was entirely inappropriate. But it did not follow from this that Möllendorff would politically ally himself with Japan.

Möllendorff became a foreign advisor of Korea because he was charged to do so by the Qing. Yet, it was his own understanding that the Qing considered Korea a "tributary." As such, it ought to be the case that "if Korea is a tributary, its domestic politics must be completely independent from Qing influence."

On this point, Möllendorff's understanding and position were thus essentially the same as that of Kim Okkyun and Denny, whose views were outlined above. However, the circumstances that Möllendorff was subjected to and the actions he took nevertheless differed greatly from those of Kim and Denny.

At the time, Korea was engaging in relations with many more countries than it had done before. Möllendorff took charge of the practical side of this diplomatic work, and in doing so, sought to construct a series of diplomatic relationships that would enable Korea to push back against Qing pressure. It was under such circumstances that Möllendorff chose to reach out to Russia.

After clashing militarily during the Kapsin Coup, Japan and Qing

China agreed to withdraw their troops from Korea following negotiations between Itō Hirobumi and Li Hongzhang. This was one of the stipulations of the so-called Convention of Tientsin of April 1885. Around the same time, Möllendorff was hard at work devising a plan to invite Russian military instructors to Korea, and eventually succeeded in extracting a form of Russian consent in this regard. However, his goals went far beyond just inviting Russian military instructors to the country. In order to enable Korea to push back against Qing influence in the country, he aimed to place Korea under Russian protection.

As soon as the Qing uncovered this plan, they were quick to determine that it would be deleterious to Qing interests. They were infuriated by Möllendorff's betrayal and immediately removed him from his post. This event is known as the first Russo-Korean secret agreement incident.

Although Möllendorff never did manage to succeed in signing a secret agreement with the Russians, the impact of his actions was far from small. Until that point, the international situation surrounding the Korean Peninsula had involved just the three countries of Japan, China, and Korea. The sudden appearance of Russia on the scene came to greatly complicate matters. However, it wasn't just Russia that would come to be involved with Korea. Other countries also sought to forge new relationships with the country as a result of the emerging Russian presence. A prime example of this was Britain. Wary of Russian action, the British preemptively occupied the Korean island of Kŏmundo around the same time.

Such developments engendered a situation in which the Qing now had far greater worries than just Japan. Indeed, they now needed to stay alert to the movements of multiple countries. Despite this development, however, the issue of keeping Korean action in check nevertheless constituted a task of the utmost importance for the Qing. Furthermore, this was also the key reason that the dynasty came to institute a much more interventionist policy in Korea henceforth.

The Emergence of Yuan Shikai

Selected for overseeing this task was Yuan Shikai, age twenty-seven. Although he would later become the first president of the Republic of China, at the time of the Imo Incident he was little more than a staff officer serving in the Qing force dispatched to Korea to quell the uprising. After this, he remained stationed in the Korean capital. When the Kapsin Coup erupted, he launched a swift and decisive attack in response, ensuring that the coup d'état came to nothing. Yuan's quick-wittedness during these events quickly brought him to the attention of Li Hongzhang, who recognized that the young Yuan had a promising future.

In September 1885, Yuan Shikai escorted the Taewŏn'gun back to Korea. After temporarily returning to China, in November of that year he was entrusted with overseeing the Qing's diplomatic and trade affairs with Korea, whereupon he returned to Seoul. In this post, he acted as Qing representative to the Korean government in the decade that followed.

Yuan Shikai was a young military man. As such, both his ideas and actions were more direct and uncompromising than the average Confucian scholar-official who served within the Qing bureaucracy. In 1885, he penned a memorandum to King Kojong upon returning the Taewŏn'gun to Seoul. Titled *Zhaijian lun* (On the Removal of Treachery), the 1885 text advocates the exposure and expulsion of individuals of a wicked nature. However, more than just an expression of Yuan Shikai's personal views, the text can also be seen as a direct statement of the Qing's position on Korea at the time.

The document begins in the following way:

There are those who furtively seek to instigate the Korean government [to join hands with Russia], stating that "Other countries would cease to belittle Korea if it were to accept Russian protection."

Here, Yuan was obviously referring to Möllendorff's plan to have Russia and Korea conclude a secret agreement. He firmly contested such an idea, stating the following:

Russia is currently seeking to deceive Korea by inverting its language, saying that it will protect Korea, rather than conquer and occupy Korea. Though Russia may call it protection, its aim is to self-indulgently swallow up Korea.

He then went on to assert the Qing's position on Korea:

Yuan Shikai (1859–1916), Qing representative to Korea

To begin with, the right to protect [a tributary] can only be possessed by the superior state [i.e., China]. Clear evidence of this was demonstrated in our suppression of the Imo and Kapsin insurrections.

He thus asserted that the "right to protect" Korea lay with the "superior state," namely, the Qing. He then stated the following:

Being a tributary of the Qing means autonomy in domestic politics and foreign affairs. That is not the case with the West. The mere receiving of annuities does not result in autonomy in domestic politics and foreign affairs, and even commodities collected become the property of the suzerain. (*Zhaijian lun*)

Yuan was thus describing the difference between a Qing "tributary" and a Western "vassal state," and concluded his document by asking which configuration was preferable for Korea.

What we should take note of here is Yuan's reference to Qing "protection" for Korea at the beginning of the document, and his reference to Korea's "tributary autonomy" at the end, and how these two points were intimately linked.

With these two points in mind, let us now explore the Qing's position at the time.

The Qing Stance and Yuan Shikai's Mission

Up until this point, the Qing had never broached the topic of "protecting" Korea. On the contrary, such an idea was perceived as a troublesome burden by the dynasty, as was evinced in the attitude it took toward the American Expedition to Korea of 1871.

However, the reason the Qing perceived the idea in such a way was because Korea had pushed the conflict upon the dynasty, rather than allowing the dynasty to come to that decision itself. Indeed, the Qing reserved the "right to protect" Korea if it chose; such a fact was an axiomatic aspect of a *zongshu* relationship that did not require explicit articulation. However, at the same time, it was entirely up to the Qing whether or not it would exercise this "right" that it reserved. No one, not even Korea, could compel it to do so.

However, Yuan Shikai's memorandum reveals that by the mid-1880s, the Qing had come to feel differently. Indeed, it now felt that an explicit articulation of both its "right to protect" Korea, and the fact that that right to protection was "exclusive to the superior state and the superior state alone," was now necessary. This was because it was faced with the reality of other countries who were now trying to come to its rescue, such as Russia.

In more concrete terms, when Korea had the prospect of Russian "protection" thrust upon it, this catalyzed the Qing into becoming more acutely aware of its exclusive "right to protect" a tributary in its position as the "superior state." Indeed, the Qing came to actively recognize anew the importance of its right to "protect" a tributary. Previously, it had taken this aspect of its *zongshu* relationships as an axiomatic feature and had avoided discussing the topic as it risked instigating some form of disorder. However, from the 1880s onwards, the Qing took a new stance on the issue. From this time onward, it was actually the Qing, rather than Korea, that actively advocated its right to "protect" its tributary.

This then raises the question: Did Qing perceptions of "tributary autonomy" shift in this period as well? While the term itself retained its pre-existing definition, the content it implied was by no means a reiteration of what had come before. Indeed, as the Qing now felt compelled to secure its "right to protect" Korea, this idea became intimately intertwined with the very notion of "tributary autonomy," serving as one of its key premises. In other words, an even greater emphasis had come to be placed upon the notion of a "tributary" that was under the "protection" of the "superior state."

With this shift in emphasis, it then became necessary for the Qing to make Russia and the Western powers aware of the Qing's exclusive right to "protect" Korea. To do this, the Qing needed to articulate its relationships with its "tributaries" in a format that was intelligible to Westerners.

This was their motive for appointing Denny, a Westerner with legal expertise, as foreign advisor to the Korean government. And, as we saw above, this ploy backfired spectacularly.

At the same time, as a further result of this shift in emphasis, the Qing came to perceive Korea's failure to seek Qing "protection" as an act that threatened the relationship between the "superior state" and its "tributary." Furthermore, the Qing also saw the Korean failure to do so as an infraction of that which had been approved by the Korean king in the official communication to the Western powers. If the Korean failure to seek Qing "protection" was predicated on Korea's "autonomy" to do as it pleased in its domestic and diplomatic affairs—an "autonomy" that the Qing now saw as a purely nominal right—then it certainly had to be suppressed.

The suppression of Korea's nominal autonomy was thus the mission tasked to Yuan Shikai. As noted above, he was entrusted with the task of overseeing Korea's diplomatic and trade affairs. The Chinese title for his role, in literal terms, conveyed the sense of a specialist mission which had been delegated to a diplomat of ministerial rank. However, he made a point of not acting like other countries' ministers did. This extended to the English translation of his title, which was that of "Resident." This was likely a reference to the British "Residents" who were stationed in the princely states of British India. In embracing such terminology, it suggested to the Western countries that he was representing the suzerain power in one of its vassals, and that Korea was a Qing protectorate.

Yuan Shikai took this stance even more blatantly in his dealings with the Korean government. He had, in the first place, already come to harbor a deep distrust of the Min regime. This was because soon after the Qing released and returned the Taewŏn'gun to Korea under Yuan's escort, the Min regime placed him under house arrest.

Yuan's deep distrust of the Min regime soon proved to be entirely justified. In August 1886, the Korean king yet again requested Russian protection, leading to a second attempt at the signing of a secret agreement between Russia and Korea.

The truth in this incident is unclear. Even at the time, there were those who speculated that the whole event was an elaborate plot that had been hatched by Yuan Shikai. At any rate, Yuan Shikai took this event as an opportunity to recommend to Li Hongzhang that the Qing should dispatch troops to Korea and depose King Kojong. In this regard, Yuan was persistent and uncompromising.

Although his recommendation was not carried out, Yuan Shikai increased the pressure on Korea in other ways. For instance, although he subsequently acknowledged that King Kojong's actions had been carried out in the name of Korean "autonomy," he criticized and applied pressure to the Koreans for the reason that these actions were not in line with "tributary autonomy" and decried them as a form of "anti-Chinese autonomy." In other words, it was a form of "autonomy" that went against the Qing. Yuan thus interfered in the domestic politics and foreign affairs of Korea at every turn (Korea was originally

Yuan Shikai's name card. "H.I.C.M. Resident" can be seen written to the left of the name.
Reproduced with permission from Okamoto Takashi, *Zokkoku to jishu no aida: Kindai Shin-Kan kankei to Higashi Ajia no meiun* [Between Dependency and Sovereignty: Modern Qing-Korean Relations and the Destiny of East Asia] (Nagoya: University of Nagoya Press, 2004).

supposed to be able to exercise "autonomy" in both of these), and even moved, in 1887, once again to dethrone King Kojong. For Denny, this was the last straw, and led to his publication of *China and Korea*.

Yuan Shikai teemed with energy and would fight whoever or whatever got in his way. When he discovered that George C. Foulk, U.S. Navy officer and acting chargé d'affaires to Korea, was a critic of his and was on intimate terms with King Kojong, Yuan had Foulk expelled from the country by intimating that there was risk of him colluding with the king. What is more, when he realized that the dispatching of permanent Korean diplomatic missions to the West could be inimical to the Qing's interests, he tried by all possible means to prevent the missions from going ahead. In this way, he created disputes at every turn.

Yuan's superior, Li Hongzhang, often reprimanded him for being thoughtless and going too far, but never dismissed him. This was because Li saw Yuan's role as indispensable.

The ultimate authority upon which Yuan relied for justifying his actions was the statement on Korea's "tributary autonomy" found in the official communication that had been sent to the Western powers. As we have seen, the term "tributary" had come to take on a greater range of meaning by this point, and was no longer taken just to mean a country that paid tribute to China and engaged in ceremonial relations with it. However, as the right to "protection" that Yuan sought to invoke took the idea of "tributary autonomy" as its underlying premise and justification, he could not sever the principle from the long-standing idea of *zongshu* relations, nor from the traditional ceremonial observances that were involved in this relationship. Furthermore, emphasizing and demonstrating the existence and reality of this *zongshu* relationship to both the Western powers and Korean government was a sine qua non for Yuan. Failing to do so would mean that his actions were entirely devoid of justification. Thankfully for him, an opportunity to do so would soon materialize.

The Dispatch of a Condolence Mission

On June 4, 1890, Shinjŏngwanghu (Queen Sinjong) of Korea passed away at the age of 83. As we have seen, she had been queen regent for King Kojong and a senior member of the Korean royal house who had lived through the reigns of four monarchs, and was the final arbiter of support for King Kojong's accession to the throne. The passing of such an individual inevitably held significant implications both for Korea and for other foreign states. It also came to exert an influence on Qing-Korean relations.

In the event that the king of a tributary state were to pass away, it was customary in traditional *zongshu* relations for the Chinese emperor to dispatch an embassy to the tributary with a letter that offered the emperor's condolences and eulogized the departed. This was referred to as a condolence mission by the Chinese. While Queen Sinjong was not a king, it was decided that a condolence mission should be dispatched, as she was a relative of the king.

Appointed as chief envoy and deputy envoy were Xu Chang and Chong Li, both bannermen in the Eight Banners (the divisions structuring the Qing socio-military system). Having received their orders on October 15, the two departed Beijing on October 30, left Tianjin on November 4, and arrived in Inchŏn by boat two days later. They entered the Korean capital on November 8 and concluded the condolence ceremonies without delay, after which they attended a banquet at their lodgings and departed Seoul on November 11. They reached Tianjin on November 16 and then reported back to the emperor in Beijing at the end of November.

Looked at in this way, it would appear that both the dispatch of the mission and the condolence ceremonies proceeded without any problems. However, this was far from what actually happened.

Yuan Shikai had already started planning the dispatch of this mission when Queen Sinjong's condition took a critical turn. Yuan was determined to use the mission as an opportunity to demonstrate to the world the proper workings of Qing-Korean relations. He worked proactively in this case, as he had previously.

By contrast, the Koreans took an exceedingly disinterested stance toward the proceedings. According to precedent, it was Korea that had to notify the Qing of Queen Sinjong's passing and request a condolence mission. And yet, it seems the Koreans were quite reluctant to send such an envoy.

That was not all. When the Korean envoy at last arrived in Beijing some three months later, he stated that there was no need for the Qing to send a condolence mission. The reason he gave was that financial difficulties would prevent Korea from being able to receive the mission with all the hospitality and pageantry that was typically expected.

The Qing naturally interpreted this as an expression of defiance and refused to accept the envoy's request to shelve the condolence mission. In order to shut the Korean excuse down, they decided to have the mission travel by steamboat, which would mean a reduction in expenses associated with the reception of the mission.

Certain routes were associated with the comings and goings of envoys in *zongshu* relations, and in the case of Korea, the precedent had always been overland travel. The introduction of the boat as the mode of transport for this particular mission would, therefore, reduce the journey time considerably. However, this switch in mode of transport also served another, ulterior purpose. Foreigners resided in the ports at which steamboats dropped anchor. Traveling by steamboat would, therefore, ensure that many foreigners would bear witness to the mission when it arrived.

Yuan Shikai explained that the reason Korea wanted to avoid receiving a mission of condolence from the Qing was because "as the foreign countries were watching it," it feared that "the dignity of its autonomous status would be damaged if it was proven, through its reception of a Qing mission, that it is a tributary of the Qing."

While we cannot be sure of the Korean government's true intentions, this was, at least, how the Qing judged the situation. What is more, the Qing determinedly moved to conduct all the actions and processes that Korea was trying to avoid. Performing these condolence missions and the related ceremonies to a foreign audience was, from the Qing perspective, essential. While Korea remained reluctant, it would eventually accede and accept the Qing mission. This was likely because Korea did not want to disavow the ceremonial act itself.

The Publication of the *Shi-Han jilüe*

Following the conclusion of the condolence mission, Yuan Shikai published a pamphlet in 1892 titled *Shi-Han jilüe* (Record of the Mission to Korea) that described the course of events in a diary format. Below, I would like to discuss two prominent features of the text and the format in which it was published.

The first is the extremely unbalanced structure of the text considering its diary format. About one-third of it is made up of descriptions of the condolence ceremonies and ceremonial procedures and rules— what we would call a "program."

Yuan did not structure the text in this way merely to keep a record of the ceremonial and ritual acts involved in the mission. Appended to the end of every entry for the days on which a ceremony had been held was, without fail, a comment by Yuan that stated that the ceremony

The *Shi-Han jilüe*, published by Yuan Shikai in 1892

had "been conducted according to plan." In affixing these comments, Yuan likely wanted not only contemporary onlookers but also history to remember that Korea had indeed performed the ceremonies that were expected of it. Indeed, the text was designed with the purpose of declaring to all that Qing-Korean relations were alive and well, and that they were being acted out in accordance with historical precedent.

The second feature is that an English version of the *Shi-Han jilüe* was published at the same time, under the title of *Notes on the Imperial Chinese Mission to Corea, 1890*. This was done, of course, so that it could be read by diplomats as well as other foreigners. This is also clear from the fact that Yuan Shikai presented a volume to the British consul general in the Korean capital of Seoul as soon as the text was ready.

Yuan stated that he published this English version of the text in the hope that it would do away with the baseless disinformation about Qing-Korean relations that foreigners had been spreading. Indeed, the text was drawn up with the aim of offering an insight into the ideal form that Qing-Korean relations should take, and its target readership was not only those who were involved in the rituals themselves but also third-party observers.

The dispatch of the condolence mission and the execution of its ceremonies were done, first and foremost, to demonstrate and make visible the Qing-Korean *zongshu* relationship to a Western audience. That being the case, we can also understand the *Shi-Han jilüe*, as a written expression of that relationship, to be a record of events that was primarily meant to be read by a Western audience. Indeed, the Qing-Korean relationship needed to be expressed not only in Chinese, but in English as well.

Between Ritual and International Law

The final entry in the *Shi-Han jilüe* is for November 14, 1890. After offering a summary of the departure of the Qing condolence mission's chief and deputy envoys from Korea, the text states the following:

> The two envoys expressed the Emperor's tender consideration for the little [country, i.e., Korea] and his desire to conciliate his tributary, which cannot but extend to the minutest of details. How wonderful! How splendid! Most magnificent!

This was a very Chinese way of expressing things. In contrast, the English version reads:

> The Emperor's consideration for his vassal state as evinced by his thoughtfulness in matters pertaining to the Mission, is fathomless. How admirable and satisfactory! And how glorious!

I will not attempt a tedious interpretation of these words. Instead, I want only to draw the reader's attention to how the term used for "tributary" (C. *shubang*, J. *zokuhō*, K. *sokpang*) here is rendered in English as "vassal state."

Besides "tributary," the *Shi-Han jilüe* uses a variety of words for Korea, variously meaning "a subjugated borderland" or even "an eastern borderland." All of these terms were rendered as "vassal state" in the English-language edition. This was not a coincidence. Rather, this consistent lexical choice can be understood as a deliberate act on the part of the Qing.

In encountering this lexical choice, we ought to cast our minds back to what Denny had argued in his *China and Korea* pamphlet. There, he wrote that the term *shuguo* or *sokkuk* should be translated as "tributary state" and not as "vassal state." The English version of *Shi-Han jilüe* took the opposite direction, instead choosing to intentionally translate "tributary state" as "vassal state."

This divergence in lexical choice is exceedingly revealing about the structure that Qing-Korean relations took at the time. In short, it reveals that the respective positions of the Qing and Korea differed in regard to how the terms "tributary" and "autonomy" (J. *jishu*, K. *chaju*) were understood.

While the Qing sought to expand the definition of "tributary" from a relationship predicated on ritual to one predicated on a more explicit form of subordination and protection, Korea wanted to keep the notion limited to the idea of ritual. Furthermore, while Korea sought to understand its "autonomy" in accordance with the notion of independence as expressed under international law, the Qing saw this "autonomy" as a purely nominal feature.

As we saw earlier, in the early 1880s, the Korean political sphere split into the Serving-the-Great Party and the Independence Party. These groups opposed each other on the basis of their respective understandings of the "tributary" and "autonomy" concepts. In less than a decade, however, this opposition had also come to manifest itself in Qing-Korean relations. What is more, these opposing sides had clearly now come to base their understanding of these concepts on two differing normative systems: Confucian systems of ritual and international law.

These opposing positions of ritual propriety and international law

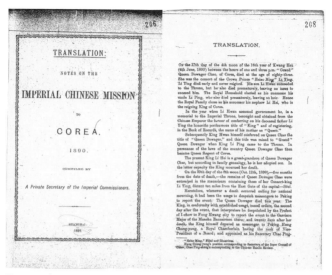

Notes on the Imperial Chinese Mission to Corea, 1890, English version of the
Shi-Han jilüe
Reproduced with permission from Okamoto Takashi, *Chūgoku no tanjō: Higashi Ajia no kindai
gaikō to kokka keisei* [The Birth of China: International Relations and the Formation of a Nation
in Modern East Asia] (Nagoya: University of Nagoya Press, 2017).

were made explicit through the *Shi-Han jilüe* and *China and Korea*. It
is important that we do not overlook the fact that, while the assertions
made were poles apart, both were published in English. That is, the
intended audience of both was foreigners, namely Westerners. The fact
that the two opposing arguments were made with a Western audience
in mind can also be interpreted as an indication that the texts' foreign
audience had yet to commit to either of the two conflicting positions.

Between the extremes of the Qing and Korea, of "tributary" and
"autonomy," and of ritual and international law, there thus existed the
common dimension of Western opinion that needed to be influenced.
This fact not only signified that the Qing-Korean relations of the 1880s
could not be reduced to mere bilateral relations between the two sides
but also suggests that the actions of Western countries conversely had
the potential to affect the nature and development the Qing-Korean
relationship.

That being the case, what actions did the Western countries and Japan take in regard to the Qing-Korean relationship at the time? In the period between the outbreak of the Imo Incident and the publication of *China and Korea* and the *Shi-Han jilüe*, how did the Western countries respond to attempts by Korea and the Qing to influence opinion? Furthermore, how did these powers exert influence on both the Qing and Korea? What were the results of these efforts? In order to consider such questions, we need to delve back in time once more.

3. The Consequences of Protecting Korea

The Plan for Korean Neutrality

For Japan, the outcome of the Imo Incident was deeply unsatisfying. In its negotiations with Korea leading up to the signing of the Chemulpŏ Treaty, it had seemingly not made any mistakes. It had treated Korea as an independent country, conducted the negotiations with the Koreans directly, and had succeeded in establishing a satisfactory set of regulations. However, unknown to the Japanese, the Qing had abducted the Taewŏn'gun, had begun to interfere in Korean domestic politics, and had come to openly take a much more hands-on approach to its Korean "tributary."

One person who witnessed these developments on the ground in Korea and was deeply worried about them was Inoue Kowashi, a member of the legislative advisory council. He was ordered to Korea on August 20, 1882, to assist Hanabusa Yoshimoto in the negotiations with the Korean government. He was involved in the negotiations leading up to the Chemulpŏ Treaty and returned to Shimonoseki, Yamaguchi Prefecture, on September 16.

From Inoue's perspective, the Qing had "put into practice their long-held ideas" and, while "arguing that tributary [status] and autonomy do not run counter to each other," the Qing were "excessively interfering" in Korean affairs in the way one "might expect in the case of a vassal state." He also stated that Japan "should truly regret having given tacit consent to the Chinese tributary claim," suggesting that he had keenly taken note of Ma

Jianzhong's definition of "tributary autonomy" and the actions to which it led.
Especially problematic for Inoue was
the fact that the Qing's "interference" in
Korean affairs had no basis in international law. This meant that it was unclear
"how much they would interfere and
when this interference would end," and
that it was impossible to gauge whether
this interference would be "permanent
or only temporary." This made it difficult
for Japan to formulate an appropriate
"course of political strategy" and a policy
for how to handle Korea.

Inoue Kowashi (1844–1895), member of
the Japanese legislative advisory council
Photo courtesy of the National Diet Library, Japan

Up until the outbreak of the Imo Inci-
dent, Inoue's position was that Japanese-Korean relations were wholly
separate from Qing-Korean relations, and that it was fine for Japan to
treat Korea as an independent country, regardless of how the Qing might
comment or respond to such a position. However, the outbreak of the
Imo Incident demonstrated that such a stance was wholly unviable, and
forced Inoue to revise his understanding of the situation.

Having done so, Inoue Kowashi drafted the *Chōsen seiryaku iken an*
(Draft Proposals for [Japanese] Policy toward Korea, 1882) upon his return
to Japan. Two key characteristics of Inoue's proposals were (a) the fact that
they took the increasing interdependence of Qing-Korean relations and
Japanese-Korean relations as a basic premise for the policy recommendations, and (b) the fact that they had been devised so as to not contradict
Japan's pre-existing interests and political stances. Let us examine an excerpt:

The five countries of Japan, Qing China, the United States, Britain,
and Germany are to meet and discuss Korea. They should regard
Korea as a neutral country, meaning that, following the examples
of Belgium and Switzerland, it will be a country that may not invade

others nor be invaded by others, and shall come under the joint protection of the five countries.

The Qing claim that they are Korea's superior state and that Korea is a Qing tributary, yet Korea is not a dependency [of the Qing]. They [the Qing] must not hinder Korea from being an independent country. Moreover, the Qing, together with the four other countries, should make [Korea] a joint protectorate, and not interfere in Korean domestic politics without first obtaining consent from the other four.

If this plan is realized, political maneuvers in the Orient will become slightly safer. Korea must, not only for the sake of Japanese interests, but for its own sake as well, gain the status of perpetual neutrality and free itself from China's yoke. Moreover, for China's sake it must fulfill its duty as a tributary by doing away with the malaise of a false reputation that does not match its actual power.

What is most important here is that this was likely the first time that a key person in the Japanese government publicly acknowledged the Qing claim to being a "superior state." The use of the term was predicated on the previously issued official communication from the Korean king about Korea's "tributary autonomy," and was arguably used by Inoue as a means to avoid a breakdown in Japan's relations with the Qing that followed, in its relations with Korea, the terms that had been laid out in the official communication.

Even so, that Inoue referred to the Qing's status as a "superior state" in its relations with Korea did not mean that he agreed that the Qing should be allowed to "interfere" with or seek to "protect" Korea. Inoue's understanding was that if Korea's ability to exercise control over its "domestic politics and foreign affairs" constituted what was meant by "autonomy," then while Korea could be a Qing "tributary" it most certainly could not be a Qing "dependency." By Inoue's definition, that meant that Korea was an "independent country."

Surprisingly, this line of thinking coincides with that of Denny and Möllendorff. Inoue's understanding of a "tributary" likely relied on the assertion in Wheaton's *Elements of International Law* that states that tribute "does not necessarily affect [a country's] independence." Even though their positions differed, it appears that they all reached the same conclusion, in terms of international law.

There was no reason for any of the Western powers to take issue with the official communication they had received from the Korean king, so long as the terms it outlined were understood according to the principles of international law. Indeed, it could even serve as a basis for developing a series of multilateral relationships that were founded upon a common understanding between the Qing, Korea, and the great powers.

However, at the same time, it was already a reality that the Qing was taking a much more interventionist role in Korea, "interfering" in its affairs and seeking to exercise their right to "protect" it. As Korea was an "independent country," such "interference" in its domestic politics was impermissible. However, at the same time, it was commonly recognized that there also existed a need to "protect" Korea, as public order had deteriorated there. As such, a solution was needed that could allow for Korea's "protection" but that simultaneously did away with the exclusivity that the Qing claimed to "interfere in" and "protect" the country.

It was then that Inoue Kowashi struck upon the idea of bringing the "five countries" who had (a) concluded treaties with Korea, and (b) found common agreement in the terms articulated in the official communication they had received from the Korean king, to "jointly protect" Korea. In doing so, they could follow "the examples of Belgium and Switzerland" by ensuring that Korea enjoyed "perpetual neutrality" that forbade any form of "interference" in its affairs.

Inoue was rather confident in this proposal, which could be termed a plan for Korean neutrality. In terms of its reasoning, the proposal was very sophisticated in that it aimed to bring legal and permanent stability to the country. Furthermore, by advocating a neutrality that would be ensured on a multilateral basis, it dealt with and offered a solution to all of the points that, as we have seen, Möllendorff, Yuan Shikai, and Denny would later take issue with. It was thus an excellent proposal for the time. However, the issue of whether it could be put into practice was another question altogether.

Beginning in November 1882, Inoue began work on implementing his proposal by approaching the Qing and the United States through the Japanese Ministry of Foreign Affairs. However, the results of these efforts did not bode well. The Qing refused to even consider the plan, instead choosing to proceed with its new interventionist policy for the country. Meanwhile, the United States and the other Western countries had yet to ratify their treaties with Korea at this point in time and were not at a stage where they could think about a program of joint "protection" for Korea nor about a plan for its "perpetual neutrality."

In short, Inoue's proposal came too early. And, before an opportune moment to reconsider its ideas could arrive, the Kapsin Coup broke out and the situation suddenly changed.

The Kapsin Coup and Korea's Actions

In essence, the Kapsin Coup constituted a power struggle between opposing Korean factions. However, the fact that it led to a military clash between Japan and the Qing brought three recondite points back into the spotlight. First was the fact that the Korean government lacked adequate military power of its own. Second was the huge significance that the Korean Peninsula held for both Japanese and Qing interests. And third was the immense influence Japan and Qing exerted on the Peninsula as well. These reasons were also heavily implicated in Japan's decision to conclude the Convention of Tientsin with Qing representative Li Hongzhang after the coup had been brought to an end.

Signed in April 1885, the Convention of Tientsin provided for a mutual withdrawal of troops from Korea, and functioned as a medium for Japan and the Qing to express their respective positions on Korea. However, from the viewpoint of other interested third parties, the treaty's stipulations did not go far enough. This was because a withdrawal of troops by both countries would be insufficient for determining if long-term stability could prevail in Korea. Sandwiched between Japan and the Qing, Korea, too, was unable to shake off its misgivings about the sort of conduct the two countries could pursue in in the future, and realized that it could no longer remain a passive observer.

The subsequent actions that Korea took were complex and are difficult to trace. However, things become clearer when we bring Inoue Kowashi's plan for Korean neutrality, and the joint form of "protection" that he had advocated, back into the picture.

The "protection" that Korea had sought up until 1882 had been wholly centered on the Qing. However, once Korea realized that this "protection" came at the price of Qing interference, the whole prospect became much less appealing. Korea therefore moved to do away with the Qing's exclusive right to its "protection," and seek it elsewhere.

The Independence Party sought out Japanese "protection," but this plan ended in failure. Meanwhile, while the Serving-the-Great Party continued to embrace Qing "protection," this failed to become a mainstream position. For Korea, the challenge of its foreign relations going forward was thus where and how to find this "protection" once it was no longer exclusively tied to the Qing. In this regard, it shared something in common with Inoue Kowashi's plan for achieving Korean neutrality.

Neutrality, Exclusive Protection, or Joint Protection?

On the question of Korean protection, around January 1885, at the time of the conclusion of the Kapsin Coup, a number of approaches were being discussed with regard to how the Korean situation could be stabilized. One particularly representative idea was the suggestion of Russian intervention.

The first of these ideas would be a proposal for Korean neutrality that was put forth by Hermann Budler, the acting German consul general in Seoul. After this came Möllendorff's request for Russian protection (which had led to the first attempt at the signing of a secret agreement between Russia and Korea).

At first glance, the two proposals appear entirely distinct. The former proposed that Korea's neutrality be guaranteed through a multilateral pact between Japan, the Qing, and Russia. Meanwhile, the latter proposed that Korea should become an exclusive Russian protectorate.

However, if we examine them closely, one realizes that the only key difference in the proposals was the question of whether or not Russia would cooperate with Japan and the Qing. Both proposals took the premise of introducing a third party into the Japan-Qing dyad, with Russia constituting that third party in both cases. In addition, both plans sought to equip Korea with the appropriate countermeasures for preventing another instance of it being overrun by a Japanese or Chinese military invasion.

Furthermore, despite their superficial differences, both of these proposals had, in fact, been based on a plan devised by Möllendorff before the Kapsin Coup. With the signing of the Convention of Tientsin, this plan, which had long remained private, suddenly came out into the open, albeit taking two alternate forms. The first of these was Budler's plan for Korean neutrality. The second of these was Möllendorff's own plan, which called for Russian protection of Korea.

Britain was particularly opposed to this kind of thinking. Long fearing a Russian southward advance, it was particularly dissatisfied by the situation that the Sino-Japanese Convention of Tientsin had created. Indeed, as Japanese and Qing troops were to withdraw from Korea, this would lead to the emergence of a military vacuum in the country. Britain had instead hoped that either Japan or the Qing would continue to offer "protection" to Korea, or that they would both do so on a joint basis. This betrayal of expectations was also highly implicated in the reasoning behind Britain's decision to occupy Kŏmundo Island for almost two years in total. Ironically, its occupation of the island had the effect of accelerating the Russian approach to Korea. With this, tensions in the region reached the boiling point.

Based on extant records, we may surmise that the Japanese, including Minister for Foreign Affairs Inoue Kaoru, were not necessarily opposed to Budler's plan for Korean neutrality. This was likely because a similar idea had already been pitched to Japan in Inoue Kowashi's proposals.

However, the prospect of Korean neutrality was eventually eliminated by events following Korea's first attempt to sign a secret agreement with Russia. A number of views existed in Korea on the best course of diplomatic policy for the country, and there were signs that a number of individuals in the country looked favorably upon Budler's plan for neutrality. However, before such opinions could be voiced in official negotiations, Korea began to show signs that it was moving to sign a secret pact with Russia, and these movements became public knowledge. Under the circumstances of the time, such actions constituted a rejection of both a potential partnership between Japan, the Qing, and Russia, and therefore of a potentially multilaterally ensured neutrality for the country. Indeed, Korea's actions indicated that it had chosen to seek out the exclusive "protection" of Russia.

For the Koreans, self-preservation was key. In that sense, whether it chose to pursue neutrality or it chose to pursue the right to exclusive Russian protection would make little difference. Both options would arguably enable it to achieve such an aim. However, for the Japanese, the prospect of a Russian military advance into Korea was far more serious. It was completely at odds with Japanese interests.

The prospect of potential collusion between Russia and Korea inspired fear in Inoue Kaoru. He therefore set about producing a memorandum titled *Chōsen benpō* (A Plan for Handling Korea, 1885) in consultation with Xu Chengzu, the Qing minister to Japan. In essence, it constituted a plan for turning Korea into a de facto joint Sino-Japanese protectorate.

At this point, the Korea question boiled down to just two viable options: exclusive or joint protection. Indeed, Inoue's plan for a multilateral alliance that would both protect and render Korea neutral was now untenable. The conditions that would enable the realization of such a plan had, for the most part, ceased to exist.

The Qing Stance

Yet the reality was that neither of these options—of exclusive or joint protection—had been achieved for Korea. And it was the actions of the Qing that played a fundamental role in this regard.

Since the signing of the Treaty of Kanghwa, Japan had taken the position that Korea was "independent." Establishing a joint protectorate with the Qing would contradict this stance, as it came down to an official recognition that the Qing had the right to engage in Korea's "protection," and to look upon Korea as a tributary or dependency. It was for this reason that Inoue Kowashi insisted that Korea should be neutral, an idea that he himself had devised. Indeed, in order to preserve Korea's continued "independence," the country had to be contained and kept neutral with the assistance of another country. Had Japan been content with establishing a standard joint protectorate with the Qing from the start, there would have been no need for it to broach the issue of Korean neutrality. A neutral Korea was thus key for the Japanese side.

Given such circumstances, it seems reasonable to infer that the reason that Inoue Kaoru presented his *Chōsen benpō* proposals to the Qing at the time was because Japan felt that the only remaining option open to it was to establish a joint Korean protectorate with the Qing. However, unfortunately for Inoue, Li Hongzhang and the Qing side rejected his proposals, meaning that a de facto joint protectorate never came to be.

The Qing rejection of Inoue's proposals meant that Japan had now lost the means for active engagement in the Korea issue. Out of respect for the terms to which it had agreed with the Qing in the Convention of Tientsin, Japan withdrew its troops from Korea. And, after this, it was left with no choice but to step back from the Korean situation.

However, in the end, the negotiations between Japan and the Qing did little for the restoration of regional stability. And, it was these lingering tensions that, one year later in 1886, ensured that the British occupation of Kŏmundo Island remained in place, and that a second attempt at signing a secret Russo-Korea agreement would be pursued. While the Qing and Li Hongzhang did indeed reject Inoue Kaoru's proposals, after the Kapsin Coup, they doubled down on their efforts at exerting direct influence over Korea, and rapidly buttressed their regional military capabilities. Examples of the former came with their removal of Möllendorff from his post and their stationing of Yuan Shikai in the country, while examples of the latter came with their formation of the Beiyang fleet in 1888. As such, they were far from passive observers of the Korea situation.

The Qing position was that Korea was a "tributary." While this term had previously constituted little more than an official position or principle, the series of events that encompassed the Convention of Tientsin negotiations, the occupation of Kŏmundo Island, and the secret agreements between Russia and Korea demanded that the Qing come to foster a conscious awareness of the meaning of what exactly this concept entailed.

As I have already discussed, the Qing argued that the protection of Korea ought to be undertaken by itself, as the "superior state." An inability to exercise this function or right would mean that the Qing would no longer be able to look upon Korea as a tributary. Giving up Korea's status as a tributary, or its own exclusive claim to Korean protection, was therefore impermissible.

This meant that the plan to construct a program of multilateral "protection" for Korea that would render it neutral and, therefore, ensure its continued "independence" was entirely out of the question. Furthermore, the Qing was also unable to endorse both the prospect of Russia taking over as Korea's exclusive "protector" (as had been attempted through the signing of the Russo-Korean secret agreement) and the idea of establishing a joint Sino-Japanese protectorate. Indeed, in order for the Qing to be able to recalibrate the terms of its own relationship with Korea, and in order for it to make these terms known internationally, such plans inevitably had to be given the cold shoulder.

The Balance of Power and "Tributary Autonomy"

Under such circumstances, the other powers with an interest in Korea feared a loss of regional stability and could not idly sit by. One such country was Russia, which had made repeated approaches toward Korea.

Objectively speaking, be it in northeast China or on the Korean Peninsula, Russia did not at that time possess military strength adequate to launching an attack on the Qing. The Trans-Siberian Railway had yet to be built, and the eastern extremities of the Russian continent were sparsely populated and suffered from labor shortages. Indeed, Russia didn't stand a chance: there was a huge gap, both in developmental terms and in terms of military preparedness, between Russia and the Qing's Three Eastern Provinces that sat on the other side of the Amur and Ussuri rivers.

The Russian government was well aware of the disadvantages it faced, and it was always very cautious about the depth to which it involved itself in affairs relating to the Korean Peninsula. That being said, this did not mean that Russia would simply allow another country, particularly Qing China, to expand the reach of its influence there. Maintenance of the status quo was absolutely key for Russia. This was why it realized that it needed to make amends with the Qing after the two countries' bilateral relationship had soured as a result of the failed signing of a secret agreement between Russia and Korea.

In 1886, the events involved in the second attempt at the signing of a secret agreement between Russia and Korea would provide the means for Russia to make amends with the Qing. Nikolai F. Ladyzhensky, Russian chargé d'affaires in Beijing, conducted secret negotiations with Li Hongzhang in Tianjin that resulted in a joint agreement on mutual nonaggression on the Korean Peninsula.

Next, there was Britain. Its sudden occupation of Kŏmundo Island suggested that the question of whether Korea was independent or autonomous was entirely immaterial for it. All that mattered was that a potential southward advance by Russia was prevented. As such, so long as a potential Russian advance was contained, Britain was content with any kind of configuration for Korea, be it multilateral protection, Japanese-Qing joint protection, or even exclusive Qing rule.

Following the second attempt at the signing of a Russo-Korean secret agreement, Britain started to openly support the Qing claim to "suzerainty" over Korea. Since both the prospect of multilateral protection for Korea and joint Sino-Japanese protection for Korea showed no sign of coming to fruition, Britain instead began to promote the formalization and substantiation of exclusive Qing rule over Korea.

However, the Qing, and Li Hongzhang in particular, had no intention of taking on the formal rule of Korea, as had been rather blatantly encouraged by Britain:

It is said that as Russia has its eyes set on Korea, the British desire us, the Qing, to launch a swift attack on Korea and to incorporate it as a land under our jurisdiction. Britain is clearly out to provoke war. . . . While Britain puts on a particularly good display of goodwill, in reality, it cares little about us.

Even if the Western countries were to regard Korea as having autonomy, they cannot openly deny that Korea is a tributary of ours, and they certainly cannot force us to deny Korea's status as a tributary. If the Korean king were to think himself mightier than he is and stopped paying tribute, the situation may change. However, until then, we cannot denounce them publicly nor penalize them with armed force. (*Qing Guangxu chao Zhong-Ri jiaoshe shiliao* [Sources Relating to Sino-Japanese Negotiations Conducted during the Guangxu Emperor's Reign of Qing China], 1932)

If the Qing were to act in such a manner, then their relations with Korea, Japan, and Russia would break down, and the situation would get out of hand. This was why the Qing, while intensifying the pressure it applied to Korea, did not enact a full-blown Western-style treatment of this tributary as a vassal state, and instead sought to emphasize its traditional *zongshu* relationship and insist upon its "tributary autonomy."

The reason this situation was sustained internationally, albeit imperfectly, was because it was undergirded by a balance of power of sorts. In the context of Japanese-Qing relations, this was the mutual withdrawal agreement that had been made as part of the terms of the Convention of Tientsin. In Russo-Qing relations, it was the agreement on mutual nonaggression that had been made between Li and Ladyzhensky. And, in Qing-Korean relations, it was the dialectical tension between "tributary" and "autonomy" that paradoxically enabled, for the most part, sustained stability.

These situations came together, in tripartite formation, to produce a balance of power that enabled the region, and the Korean Peninsula, to remain stable. At the heart of such a balance of power was, in Li Hongzhang's words, "self-restraint." While the Qing enjoyed a superior position in each of these three relationships, it refrained from exercising military force so as to keep its relations with the other parties on amicable terms. As a result, the Korean Peninsula became a military vacuum and achieved a status of near-neutrality.

However, from an outsider's perspective, things would have appeared quite different. The principle of "tributary autonomy" was difficult to understand through the prism of international law. What is more, as the Li-Ladyzhensky Agreement had been negotiated in secret, it remained relatively recondite. Achieving an improvement in the instability that had mired the region in the wake of the signing of the Sino-Japanese Convention of Tientsin would have seemed highly unlikely as well. This was reflected in how the debate over "tributary" and "autonomy" raged on between the Qing and Korea, and how foreigners with little understanding of the debate found it difficult to favor one over the other.

However, looked at in another way, it was precisely this middle ground, in which third parties committed to neither side of the debate, that enabled Korea to, in effect, enjoy a form of de facto neutrality. From a third-party perspective, the fact that a singular and unified definition did not exist for what constituted a "tributary" and what constituted "autonomy" was extremely perplexing. However, this situation also came to symbolize the delicate international situation at the time, which, while unstable, managed to escape meltdown.

CHAPTER FOUR

Independent Autonomy

1. War between Japan and the Qing

Curzon's Travels

Post–World War I Europe saw the collapse of the empires of Germany, Austria, and Russia, and the independence of many Eastern European countries. The largest of these was Poland, and any good historical map will show that, in the year 1920, something called the Curzon Line ran within its borders. It was drawn by British foreign secretary George N. Curzon to serve as a line of demarcation between Poland and Russia.

Curzon was an Asia expert who hailed from an elite British background. Before becoming British foreign secretary, he served as viceroy of the British territories in India and, in his youth, had traveled the world many times. He had keenly observed East Asia in the late nineteenth century and had penned a travelogue titled *Problems of the Far East: Japan, Korea, China*, published in 1894. There, we find the following excerpt:

> Judged, therefore, by its results prior to the war, it might be said that the policy of Li Hung Chang [Li Hongzhang], however little shaped by the canons either of logic or international custom, was unsuccessful. Each logical *faux pas* was in the end retrieved by some practical advantage. If he declined to punish Korea in the first place for her attacks upon missionaries and foreigners, he thereby escaped responsibility for her cruelties. If he allowed Korea, a vassal state of China, to make treaties with foreign powers, he at the same time vindicated his right to appear as go-between—a capacity in which

Japan was most anxious to figure. By these means he might claim to have enlisted the interest of foreign Powers as a set-off to the only two rivals whom China seriously fears in Korea, viz. Japan and Russia.

What Curzon meant by "little shaped by . . . logic or . . . custom" was the "tributary autonomy" of Korea that was so incomprehensible under international law. Elsewhere, he refers to this as a form of "diplomatic . . . indecision" on the part of the Qing and as an "anomal[y]." However, Curzon was not out to criticize Qing policy. Rather, he evaluated it positively, praising the Qing for extracting "practical advantage" from the situation. Curzon's flagging of these more subtle details thus demonstrates that the text was a competent attempt at capturing, from the contemporary British perspective, the key features of the "policy of [Li Hongzhang]" and the structure of Qing-Korean relations.

British foreign secretary George N. Curzon (1859–1925)
Photo from World History Archive/Newscom/ Kyodo News Images

Curzon had traveled the Far East in 1892. That was about a half-century after the Western powers had emerged as a key political force in East Asia, and some twenty years after they had begun direct interactions with Korea. It was also about a decade after they had concluded their first treaties with the country.

Prior to this, the East Asian order that centered around the Korean Peninsula comprised three distinct bilateral relationships: the relationship between Japan and the Qing, the relationship between the Qing and Korea, and the relationship between Japan and Korea. The arrival of the West had thrown the region's long-term stability into disarray, and had compelled its participants to embark upon a course of domestic and diplomatic reconfiguration. Curzon's travels in 1892 coincided with a period in which some measure of stability had finally been restored to the region following a prolonged period of trial and error.

The Fate of Korea's Ambiguous Position

I have previously referred to this period of stability as Korea's era of being "between tributary and autonomy." While this particular framing of mine draws upon the sort of language that was being used at the time, the situation can be expressed in other ways as well. If we were to use a more modern, albeit slightly exaggerated set of concepts, we could also say that it was a period in which Korea was "between protection and independence" or, depending on our focus, "between ritual and international law."

In any case, the reason Korea's situation at the time is difficult to express is because it cannot be contained in our thinking and vocabulary. This shows how much we are today caught up in the concepts, or biases, of Western modernity.

In any event, at the time, Korea subsisted in what we might understand to be an interstitial or intermediate space that prevented it from being wholly subsumed under either the distinction of "tributary" or "protectorate," or the distinction of "autonomous" or "independent." This ambiguity also gave rise to a balance of power of sorts that, in turn, helped ensure regional stability.

However, at the same time, this interstitial space that Korea occupied was, ideologically speaking, nothing more than a middle ground. It was a vacuum that had been created by a series of overlapping bilateral deadlocks, occurring simultaneously both by chance and for a limited time. It had emerged as a result of many years of conflict and of attempts at mutual obstruction between parties of differing ideological stances.

However, it was also true that none of these parties had actively sought, as a target or aim, to bring about a comfortable ambiguity surrounding Korea's precise status in the first place. As such, this ambiguous position that Korea occupied was an unstable configuration that was highly susceptible to change, and the stability it brought to regional order lasted but a decade.

Looking back at the period today with the benefit of hindsight, it is evident to see that a new age had already begun to unfold in the region in the early 1890s.

It is known all too well how the resignation of Otto von Bismarck as chancellor of the German Empire destabilized the international political situation of the time. At around the same time in the East, the military port and batteries of Lüshun were completed, and the Qing's railways were extended beyond the Shanhai Pass in the direction of Liaodong. While these two developments on either side of the Eurasian continent had no direct correlation, both were seen as highly significant in Russian eyes.

Bismarck's stepping down led to the nonrenewal of the so-called Reinsurance Treaty between Germany and Russia, and the fortification of Liaodong caused Russia to worry about the Far East. These respective developments encouraged Russia to seek rapprochement with France and to build the Trans-Siberian Railway, and these two projects later came together with the underwriting of Russian government bonds by French capital. In turn, these developments aroused the fears of Britain and Japan, who were worried about a potential Russian southward advance. This created a situation in which the transnational to-and-fro of political ripples sent between Europe and the Far East came to be unequivocally impacted by Russia as well. At the center of many of these transnational intrigues was the question of the Korean Peninsula and its future status. And, in time, the international political situation would become so tense as to threaten the viability of Korea's ambiguous condition.

The Grain Export Prohibition Incident

Crucial in this situation were the actions of the Qing, who held in every way a superior position on the Korean Peninsula. We should pay special attention to the actions of Yuan Shikai. In his thorough faithfulness to the mission he had been given, he worked to demonstrate that Korea was a "tributary." It is hard to believe that these efforts would yield the hoped-for outcomes. Even so, Yuan never despaired. When diplomacy did not work, he continued to work tirelessly in all directions, such as trade, finance, and much more.

Yuan's efforts were not in vain. He finally saw some positive signs in 1893. The turning point was the grain export prohibition incident between Korea and Japan.

The grain export prohibition was a temporary order that was issued by local officials in Korea. Such orders were frequently issued following bad harvests and had little to do with trade in particular. The prohibition issued in Hamgyŏng Province in October 1889 followed this precedent.

To begin with, the principal product that Japan imported from Korea was rice, and the Japanese-Korean trade regulations stipulated that the implementation of a grain export prohibition should be preceded by a notice to Japanese authorities a month in advance. This time, however, the Japanese filed a formal complaint because Korea's notice had been issued less than a month in advance. Although the prohibition itself was repealed the following January, the prohibition on transactions during that time caused big losses for Japanese traders engaged in soybean exports. The pursuit of compensation for these losses became a problem at the ministerial level where the Japanese government conducted negotiations with the Korean government.

Even so, this was nothing more than an economic issue between Japan and Korea. What elevated it to the status of a major diplomatic issue was the Japanese government's decision to send a politician named Ōishi Masami to serve as its resident minister in Seoul in 1892.

Ōishi was thirty-seven at the time and was a political commentator of the Liberal Party persuasion. He had an interest in the Korea issue but was a complete novice when it came to diplomatic work. In the newly established Imperial Diet, the Liberal Party was causing trouble for the Japanese government with its attacks on the government's compromise-oriented Korea policy. The grain export prohibition incident further contributed to the problem. Ōishi's appointment as minister in Seoul was really a result of prioritizing such domestic considerations. Thus, there was a degree of surprise abroad over this particular personnel decision. The Qing and Yuan Shikai were especially put on their guard.

Yuan had initially done nothing more than observe the conflict over the grain export prohibition between Japan and Korea. It was only after Japan dispatched Ōishi as minister to Korea that Yuan suddenly started interfering in negotiations between the two countries. The official reason was that the negotiating authorities in Korea had requested his advice. Yet the problem for Yuan himself was Ōishi's very presence.

In an 1891 text titled *Fukyō saku* (Measures for Wealth and Power), Ōishi wrote the following:

If we wish to achieve Korean independence, Japan must become a leader of the Orient and convene a conference of the great powers that are most intimately engaged with the region so as to reach an agreement on the country's independence. Those that should participate in the meeting are the seven great powers of Japan, Britain, France, Russia, China, Germany, and the United States. These seven great powers should make Korea a protectorate, so that if one were to try to take Korea for itself, it should be punished by the other powers. If this at least were implemented, it would immediately ensure the firm stability of Korean independence.

To the Qing, making Korea a "protectorate" through a "conference of the great powers" signified a repudiation of the country's "tributary autonomy" that could not be overlooked. This made Ōishi what one might call a "person of interest" to the Qing. Yuan confirmed this on-site in Korea and reported back to the Qing that "Ōishi has gone so far as to tell the Korean king that Korea will surely gain autonomy if it allies itself with Japan." It is unclear whether what Yuan reported was fact or not, but what is clear is that he thought it was true, and that he acted in accordance with that belief.

If it had been Ōishi speaking only for himself or even just on Japan's behalf, it would have been less of an issue. But the concern was that Ōishi might "ally" Japan with the Western countries and have them support Korean "autonomy," which Korea might have welcomed. Thus, Ōishi had to be ousted. The most expedient way to do so was to aggravate the pending grain export prohibition issue, pit Japan and Korea against each other, and sully Ōishi's reputation.

Ōishi was a man of brusque temperament. He adopted a rude, intimidating negotiation style from beginning to end, ignoring all forms of diplomatic etiquette and protocol, which was much disliked by the Korean government. This was a boon for Yuan Shikai, who could effortlessly take advantage of this ill will to escalate the antagonism between Japan and Korea. Matters went so far that Ōishi eventually proposed the use of military force and submitted an ultimatum to the Korean side.

The Meaning of the Incident

That the impending crisis was somehow averted was thanks to contact and coordination between Japan and the Qing, that is, between Japanese prime minister Itō Hirobumi and Li Hongzhang, superintendent of trade for the northern ports. The Korean government agreed to pay compensation upon the latter's recommendation, thus settling the grain export prohibition incident for the time being.

This conclusion, which at first glance appears to have satisfied Japanese demands, was actually a major crossroads. The reason for the Japanese government's dispatch of Ōishi was to break the deadlock in the difficult negotiations, a move intended neither to complicate the incident nor to clash with the Koreans. However, in that case, the selection of Ōishi was itself a poor decision. This is evident from Ōishi's prompt dismissal after the incident was settled, and his being replaced with Ōtori Keisuke, who concurrently served as minister in Beijing. The fact that its actions would upset the Koreans to such an extent that a final rapprochement would necessitate Qing assistance was undoubtedly an unexpected outcome for the Japanese. One wonders to what extent the Japanese government was at the time aware of the significance of such an outcome.

The reason one ponders such a question is because the outcome was a major victory for Yuan Shikai. Considering the thoroughness of everything he did, he might have resisted the idea of his superior Li Hongzhang compromising with Itō Hirobumi back home. Nevertheless, he not only accomplished Ōishi's resignation but also caused relations between Korea and Japan to deteriorate. Yuan furthermore succeeded in improving relations between himself and the Korean government, which had been tense since his arrival. In 1882, Ma Jianzhong had formulated the same equation: that a worsening of Japanese-Korean relations meant an improvement of Qing-Korean relations.

As might be expected, the basis for this was personal connections. At the time, just as Ma Jianzhong had Kim Hongjip and Cho Yŏngha, so Yuan Shikai had Min Yŏngjun. As his name suggests, Min Yŏngjun was a member of the Min clan and had previously also served as minister to Japan. The records say that he "respected and trusted" Yuan, but we obviously cannot take this at face value. Min Yŏngjun had his own motives for approaching Yuan.

In any event, the very fact that such a person as Min Yŏngjun wielded power in Korean politics was to Yuan the fruit of tireless labor and a turn for the better. The presence of Min Yŏngjun was also what allowed Yuan to give detailed instructions to the Korean government during the negotiations over the grain export prohibition issue and achieve the outcome that he had hoped for. Yet this was not all.

The Tonghak Movement and the Dispatch of Qing Troops
It was at precisely this time that the Tonghak Movement was gradually growing more intense. Tonghak was named in contrast to Western learning (i.e., Christianity). It was a new Korean religion that was based on Confucianism but also syncretized Buddhism, Taoism, and folk religion. Its founder Ch'oe Cheu started proselytizing in 1860 but was

soon persecuted and executed. Tonghak subsequently spread as a secret society. A major meeting of Tonghak was held in Poŭn County, Ch'ungch'ŏng Province, in May 1893, in which participants met in secret. They criticized the government and advocated the expulsion of foreigners, and disobeyed the authorities' orders to disperse. Not knowing what else to do, the Korean government dispatched Minister of Finance Ŏ Yunjung with instructions to pacify the situation.

The Korean government feared that the Tonghak Movement might take anti-foreign action. In order to prevent that from happening, it decided to use armed force in an unrestrained clampdown on participants. Yet the Korean state's own military power was insufficient for this purpose, so there were those that called for foreign military assistance, and Yuan Shikai was also secretly approached in this regard.

However, the majority opinion in the Korean government was that it had to be cautious about requesting assistance. Yuan Shikai was also aware of this and so did not actively show a willingness to dispatch troops. Yet he did not deny the possibility of doing so, either.

Indeed, military assistance was what Yuan wanted. It would visibly demonstrate Qing protection of Korea, thereby proving Korea's status as a "tributary." Yuan responded that the Korean government should formally request Qing military assistance if the Korean government came to find the situation intolerable. Since the Qing affirmed Korean "autonomy," at least nominally, the request for assistance had to be proactively lodged by the Korean government. What is important to take note of here is the fact that Yuan explained this process to none other than his confidant, Min Yŏngjun. One could say Yuan was laying the groundwork for the dispatch of Qing troops that was to come.

The gathering in Poŭn ended without incident, thanks to Ŏ Yunjung's carrot-and-stick persuasion. However, Tonghak adherents led by the iconoclast Chŏn Pongjun started an uprising in Chŏlla Province in March 1894, leading to the movement becoming a rebellion in both name and fact. The forces sent to quell the rebels proved practically useless, whereupon military assistance from the Qing was finally requested in mid-May, following "the precedents of the Imo and Kapsin Incidents."

As the Qing's protection of its tributary had been a cherished desire of Yuan Shikai, this was the chance of a lifetime. Yuan had Min Yŏngjun strongly recommend to the Korean government that it request Qing assistance. With reports of the fall of Chŏnju on May 31, the situation demanded action, and on June 3, the Korean government formally requested, in writing, military assistance from Yuan.

Yuan must have felt a great sense of accomplishment at that moment: everything had gone perfectly according to his plans. So much so, in fact, there were even those who speculated that the Tonghak Rebellion itself had been plotted and incited by him. While there is no evidence to suggest that this was indeed the case, such rumors go to show just how in line these developments were with Yuan's own wishes.

Since Yuan's appointment to the country, the protection that Korea desired of the Qing had been of a very different nature from that which the Qing had wanted to provide. Korea's approach to the notion of "autonomy" and the Qing's approach to the notion of "tributary" were not easy ideas to reconcile. The decade that Yuan spent in Korea was a daily struggle with that dilemma.

However, he had now, at long last, resolved this contradiction. The previously divergent Qing and Korean views on Korean protection had now come to align, with the right to exercising military protection of Korea being returned to the Qing in both name and substance. This was evident in how the Qing explained their dispatch of military assistance to Korea as being in accordance with its "precedents for protecting tributaries or borderlands under Qing jurisdiction." The Qing had long waited to be able to state this position officially, and that time was now.

As soon as Li Hongzhang received word from Yuan Shikai, he dispatched two cruisers, which reached Inch'ŏn on June 5, 1894. Moreover, 2,400 soldiers landed at Asan between June 8 and 12, followed by a further reinforcement of another 400 soldiers on June 25.

However, the rebellion itself came to an end before the Qing troops were even ready to take action. On June 10, the Chŏnju Peace Settlement was concluded between the Tonghak Movement and the Korean government, with the government accepting almost all of the rebels' demands and Chŏlla Province coming under the self-governance of the peasants.

At this rate, the Qing's dispatch of military assistance would become utterly meaningless and it would soon be forced into withdrawal. Yet something unexpected happened on that same June 10, which bewildered Yuan and deprived him of the sense of accomplishment he had hitherto enjoyed. It was the arrival of the Japanese army in Seoul.

The Japanese Dispatch of Troops

The Convention of Tientsin—within which the mutual withdrawal of Japanese and Chinese troops was stipulated—was a fairly simple agreement of three articles that was signed in 1885 to conclude the Kapsin Coup. The most important of these was Article III, which regulated future troop dispatches. It stated that if there arose a major disturbance in Korea that necessitated the dispatch of Japanese or Qing troops, the parties were required to notify each other in advance.

The text of Article III seems to suggest that should one of the parties—be it Japan or the Qing—dispatch troops, the other would merely receive a notification to that effect, and it gives no indication that the other party would be automatically entitled to do so as well. However, based on their understanding of the situation at the time, other countries interpreted this article to mean that if either Japan or the Qing dispatched troops, the other party would automatically do the same. And, while it was not stipulated in the convention, Japan and the Qing were perfectly cognizant of this interpretation as well. Indeed, this implicit aspect of the article had also played a direct role in Li Hongzhang's refraining from invoking military force in Korea.

Yuan Shikai was naturally aware of this state of affairs. That he nonetheless planned to send Qing troops to Korea at the time was because he thought the Japanese were in no position to send their own troops. This was because the Japanese political situation was marked by an ongoing antagonism between the government and the Imperial Diet. Yuan's perception of this situation led to a series of careless subsequent actions that were overly optimistic with regard to Japan. It would perhaps be more accurate to say that the Japanese reaction was far swifter than he had anticipated.

At the time, Ōtori Keisuke, the Japanese minister in Seoul, was back in Japan on a leave of absence from his diplomatic post. During this period, the legation's first secretary Sugimura Fukashi was entrusted with the discharging of its affairs. Sugimura learned of the request that the Korean government had lodged with Yuan Shikai for the provision of Qing troops and sent an emergency telegram to Japan. At a cabinet meeting on June 2, the Japanese government responded by deciding that a mixed brigade should be deployed in case of a dispatch of Qing troops. The Imperial General Headquarters was established on June 5. Ōtori left for Korea the same day, returning to his post on June 10. On that day, a 430-man Japanese naval brigade also entered the Korean capital. By this point, the Japanese army had already finished its preparations for mobilization, meaning that a mixed brigade of four thousand men landed in Inch'ŏn on June 16. This was only four days after the Qing army's arrival in Korea.

Japanese foreign minister Mutsu Munemitsu (1844–1897)
Photo courtesy of the National Diet Library, Japan

The stipulation, as per the Convention of Tientsin, regarding the delivery of a notification when a dispatch of troops had been made, was followed by both powers on June 7. This was when the Qing announced that their own dispatch of troops was in accordance with its "precedents for protecting tributaries." The Japanese cited the regulations for protecting foreign missions as per the Chemulp'o Treaty as the legal basis for their own troop dispatch. Of course, that was not the only reason for the Japanese move to deploy its troops. All things considered, the aim of the Japanese deployment was, in the words of Foreign Minister Mutsu Munemitsu, "to maintain the balance of power."

The prevailing perception was that this balance long had been in the Qing's favor. This meant that the Qing's dispatch of troops inspired in the Japanese a sense of crisis that the balance might become even more lopsided in the Qing direction and vitiate Japanese interests.

If so, Japan had to restore the "balance of power," or there would be no point in having sent troops. Until that objective was accomplished, the Japanese troops could not be withdrawn.

The Outbreak of War

Japan had dispatched its troops to Korea, and those troops showed no signs of withdrawing. This truly bewildered Yuan Shikai. The Tonghak Rebellion was already over, so it stood to reason that neither Japan nor the Qing had any reason to keep troops there. It was at this point that Yuan and Ōtori Keisuke began to negotiate a mutual withdrawal. Although they tentatively reached an agreement, it would eventually fall through.

The agreement failed because the Japanese legation feared that a mutual withdrawal would only serve to expand Qing influence in Korea, and would thus be detrimental only to Japan. That judgment was not necessarily misplaced: the Qing would consistently demand a simultaneous mutual withdrawal as a primary prerequisite in later negotiations. This was a clear sign that the Qing recognized that it stood to gain much from such an outcome.

Meanwhile, the Japanese government devised a new policy for stamping out the sort of Korean domestic conflict that that had previously invited the deployment of troops from abroad. The idea was for Japan and the Qing to direct Korean domestic political reform; if the Qing resisted this, then Japan was to instigate reform in Korea unilaterally.

This was telegraphed to the Japanese legation in Seoul, and the Qing were also notified. However, the response that the Japanese received from the Qing still prioritized a joint withdrawal. In response, Mutsu Munemitsu informed the Qing that the Japanese troops would by no means withdraw. This notification by Mutsu was made on June 22. It would be the foreign minister's first letter to the Qing, and one that proclaimed a severing of diplomatic ties.

At this time, the Japanese authorities in Korea were at a loss about what to do. The Korean government faction in favor of domestic political reforms was extremely weak, while those sympathizing with the Qing and Yuan Shikai had an overwhelming advantage. Thus, there was no chance of reform unless the Qing army was expelled, at the very least. Yet since the Qing and Japan had dispatched their troops under different pretexts, and since the Qing army was in Asan while the Japanese army was in Inch'ŏn, there was no theoretical or geographical reason for the two to clash.

If this situation were to persist, these Japanese authorities would be unable to accomplish either Korean political reform, which they were under instructions from Tokyo to carry out, or the Japanese goal of achieving a "balance of power." They somehow had to create an opportunity for the two armies to clash.

It was here that Ōtori took the advice of Sugimura and others to suddenly bring up the matter of the *zongshu* relationship between the Qing and Korea. That is, he asserted that the presence of the Qing army in Korea for the purpose of "protecting its tributary" was a violation of Article I of the Treaty of Kanghwa, which stipulated Korean "autonomy."

On July 20, Ōtori submitted an ultimatum to the Korean government, requesting that it expel the Qing army that was "violating the autonomy and independence" of Korea. If the Korean government could not remove the Qing army, then the Japanese army would. Based between Inch'ŏn and Seoul, the Japanese army advanced south to fight the Battle of P'ungdo Island on July 25 and the Battle of Sŏnghwan or Asan on July 29. The First Sino-Japanese War had finally started.

Korean "Tributary Autonomy" and War between Japan and the Qing

Given this sequence of events, it would be reasonable for the reader to conclude that the Qing-Korean *zongshu* relationship was not the primary cause of the outbreak of the war, but rather just a convenient pretext for Japan to open hostilities. Yet we must not forget that it was the Qing who had long enjoyed a dominant position in Korea up until the outbreak of hostilities, and that the basis for that dominance had been the *zongshu* relations that defined Korea as a Qing "tributary."

This held true even after the start of armed conflict. Seen objectively, what stood in the way of the "balance of power" that Japan aimed for was nothing other than the Qing's *zongshu* relationship with Korea, which gave rise to its dominant position in the country and justified the presence of its army. In order to resolve this situation, Japan had no choice but to invoke military force to eradicate both the Qing army and Qing-Korea *zongshu* relations.

Hitherto, the Qing and Korea had possessed differing understandings of the notions of "tributary" and "autonomy," the two defining features of both the Qing-Korea *zongshu* relationship and Korea's "tributary autonomy." It had been possible for Korea's status to remain somewhat ambiguous precisely because these notions had resisted taking on a uniform definition until this point, and this ambiguity functioned as a buffer against military action as well. However, Yuan Shikai, who had a great distaste for this ambiguity, had schemed to bring about a uniform definition for the notion of "tributary" and to do so by means of military action, something that the Qing had previously refrained from pursuing.

While the invocation of military might by the Qing might have personally signified mission accomplished for Yuan, objectively speaking, it also meant the destruction of the status quo and the loss of the military buffer function provided by Korea's ambiguous status. The interstitial space that Korea had once inhabited between "tributary" and "autonomy" disappeared, leaving in its wake only an ambiguity surrounding the lingering concept of "tributary autonomy," and forcing those on the ground in Korea to choose between either "tributary" or "autonomy."

Both the fact that Ōtori Keisuke's ultimatum called for the fulfillment of Korean "independence" and "autonomy," and the fact that Japan finally went to war over the issue of Korea's *zongshu* relations with the Qing—who relied on the idea of "tributary"—could perhaps be construed as a pretext or means to an end if the subject were limited to either Japanese domestic politics or the sequence of historical events at the time of the outbreak of hostilities.

However, as we have seen, if we take into account the nature of the relationship and its evolution over a longer time span, Japan's casus belli, however desperate and lacking in government-wide consensus, instead offers us a very clear indication of the nature of the situation at the time.

Interference from the Great Powers

The implications of the outbreak of the Sino-Japanese War extended far beyond the immediate context of just China, Japan, and Korea. Indeed, the outbreak of hostilities also brought a sudden shift in the positions taken on the situation by many of the great powers, who had been heavily implicated in the creation and maintenance of Korean ambiguity.

One of the factors that had enabled an enduring status quo for Korean "tributary autonomy" had been the Russian stance. The Russians supported Korean "autonomy," yet had also reached a degree of accord with the Qing (who continued to assert Korea's "tributary" status) about mutual nonaggression with regard to the Korean Peninsula.

When Japanese-Qing relations were on the verge of collapse, Li Hongzhang made use of this agreement with the Russians to request its good offices in mediating the crisis. However, all the Russian authorities did was to offer only the initial recommendation that Japan should agree to a joint withdrawal, and they took no further action when the situation took a turn for the worse. After all, Russia's interest lay in "maintaining the status quo" on the Korean Peninsula, and Russia anticipated that war might bring about change. Russia thus decided to take a back seat and observe how the situation developed, at least for the time being.

By contrast, Britain feared that Russia might take advantage of the outbreak of hostilities between Japan and the Qing to launch a southward advance. It was for this reason that Britain repeatedly urged both countries to agree to a ceasefire. This likewise had the aim of maintaining the status quo on the Korean Peninsula. To begin with, Britain had supported increased Qing intervention in Korean affairs and the dynasty's attempt to render Korea more subservient. From the British perspective, this would serve as a means to deter a Russian southward advance. Yet after the outbreak of the Sino-Japanese War, Britain came to have misgivings about the inferior power of the Qing when war broke out, and eventually moved to acknowledge and accept Japanese claims and actions.

The interference of Russia and Britain came in response to requests lodged by Li Hongzhang to the two powers. He knew full well that the power of the Beiyang army was lacking and wanted to find some way of avoiding a catastrophe. Even so, Li continued to push for a simultaneous withdrawal of Japanese and Qing troops and for the Korean government itself to implement domestic political reform. He never compromised on the assertion that Korea was a Qing "tributary."

Seen as a subjective policy, Li's aims were tantamount to an attempt at restoring the regional "balance of power" and the Korean "tributary autonomy" of the 1880s. However, in many ways, such aims were quite contradictory: the Sino-Japanese War had, after all, come about precisely as a result of the Qing themselves going against this very policy, and such an aim stood no chance of being achieved. This was because "tributary" and "autonomy" had already become a set of concepts that were mutually incompatible with the "balance of power." This is also the reason that Russia and Britain, who prioritized the "balance of power" over everything else, had already severed their respective affiliations to either the "tributary" or "autonomy" concept by this stage.

Meanwhile, Mutsu Munemitsu pushed forward with a diplomatic policy that made the first move both militarily and diplomatically. This facilitated the elimination of British and Russian interference and allowed Japan to plunge straight into unbridled warfare with the Qing. The adoption of such a strategy was very much contingent upon the shifting mood toward the Korea question adopted by Russia and Britain at the time. Mutsu's "second letter concerning the severance of diplomatic ties," so called in his 1896 *Kenkenroku* memoirs, was sent to the Qing government on July 12, and is a text that can be said to reflect the aforementioned circumstances quite well:

> Recently, out of courtesy to the friendly feelings Britain harbors toward Japan and China, the British minister to your country has invoked his good offices to act as a mediator between Japan and the Qing. He has worked to mediate the dissension between Japan and the Qing, yet the Qing government brings nothing to the discussion other than the demand that we should withdraw our troops from Korea. Does this not mean that the Qing government enjoys stirring up meaningless trouble?

As noted above, Japan's course of action was based on a denial of both Korea's pre-existing "tributary autonomy" and the pre-existing "balance of power." This then necessitated the design of a new order on the Korean Peninsula. What exactly did Japan have in mind?

2. The Kabo Reforms and the Royal Refuge in the Russian Legation

Implementing Domestic Political Reforms

On July 23, 1894, the Japanese, having deemed that no satisfactory response would come from the Korean government with regard to the final memorandum they had sent three days earlier, decided to send troops into Kyŏngbok Palace and commence a reorganization of the Korean government itself. The Japanese took this action because they judged that the general consensus on the part of the Koreans was that the Qing had the upper hand, meaning that normal diplomatic negotiations would lead nowhere.

In short, the Japanese launched a kind of coup d'état. Yet even if they were to organize a new government, there were almost no Korean officials capable of cooperating with the Japanese to implement political reforms. Therefore, the Japanese turned to the so-called moderate reformers, such as Kim Hongjip, Kim Yunsik, and Ŏ Yunjung to aid them in their task. That is, they appointed those officials who had been shunned by the government since the Kapsin Coup for being too close to the Qing. With these men on their side, the Japanese then moved to expel key people from the Min regime, and to organize a new government. This was the start of the Kabo Reforms, which fulfilled the Japanese demand for political reform.

From the Japanese perspective, initially, the idea of Korean domestic political reform was nothing more than an expedient for going to war with the Qing. Such a perspective was aptly conveyed by Mutsu Munemitsu, who stated that political reform in Korea was "not particularly crucial" and "without any significance outside of political necessity."

Nevertheless, having once been announced on the international stage, the policy had to be implemented, and once the war appeared won, the Japanese shifted to engaging more earnestly with the project. Moreover, these reforms could not have taken place without the execution of a coup d'état backed by Japanese military force; in other words, they proceeded only because of the application of Japanese pressure. The Kabo Reforms and the administration implementing them were from the outset a response to Japanese needs and dependent on Japanese military power.

Of course, the individual viewpoints and intentions of those Korean officials who had responded to the Japanese call for collaboration and who had subsequently assisted the Japanese in the Kabo Reforms were something else again. Indeed, they by no means celebrated the Japanese presence with any sincerity. However, they nonetheless sought Korean independence in their own idiosyncratic ways, and wanted to see the country achieve reform. Having been unable to achieve their longstanding goals under the Min regime, and having now borne witness to an unprecedented crisis for the country, these officials had no choice but to take charge of the situation with Japanese support, even if that meant going against their own principles.

After Kim Hongjip became chief state councillor (i.e., prime minister) in late July 1894, wide-ranging political, economic, and social reforms were intermittently implemented over the following one-and-a-half years. Some stemmed from earlier ideologies and trends, while others were introduced for the first time.

Even just a simple adumbration helps to give a sense of how the reforms were applied across the board, running the gamut from administrative organizations to some of the key systems underpinning Korean society. Indeed, there was a reorganization of government bodies, a reform of the appointment system for officials (which had hitherto centered around civil service examinations), the introduction of a modern school system, reforms for military and policing, the

Japanese foreign minister Inoue Kaoru (1836–1915)
Photo courtesy of the National Diet Library, Japan

introduction of a local governance system, reform of the tax system, the adoption of a unified currency and system for weights and measures, and a reform of the systems pertaining to social status in Korean society (the abolition of slavery, the emancipation of serfs, etc.). In the domain of Korean foreign affairs, agreements such as the Regulations for Maritime and Overland Trade between Chinese and Korean Subjects were torn up, the Qing calendar ceased to be employed in Korean diplomatic correspondence, and other measures that openly denied Korea's status as a "tributary" of the Qing were introduced. Their historical significance went far beyond mere paper reforms.

All the same, these Kabo Reforms were not free from Japanese pressure. In particular, after Inoue Kaoru took over from Ōtori Keisuke as minister to Seoul in October 1894, the pace of reform accelerated, and Korean submissiveness toward Japan became more pronounced. As an example, the Korean royal court was cut off from the government and forbidden from interfering with state administration, an action which was vehemently opposed by King Kojong and Queen Min. This move to strip the Korean royal court of its power would engender many problems in the future.

Inoue Kaoru was minister of foreign affairs at the time of the Imo Incident and the Kapsin Coup and served again in this post in the first Itō Cabinet. He continued to serve as cabinet minister thereafter as well, indicating that he was a prominent figure who normally would not have been appointed to serve as a diplomat in a legation role. That such an elite figure was appointed to a ministerial post is indicative of the extraordinary Japanese determination at the time.

Inoue himself was well aware of the exceptional circumstances that had placed a man of his caliber in such a role, and this gave him the self-confidence to forcefully push forward with Korean reform. Subsequently, a rapid succession of orders was given and there appeared to be considerable progress. But this apparent progress came about only through Japanese military power and pressure, and Japan's victories in the First Sino-Japanese War. Almost all of these policy measures were opposed from all sides in Korea, and were starting to stall. Thus, once the shared sense of Japanese military superiority began to waver in the country, both the project of achieving Korean "independent autonomy" (J. *dokuritsu jishu*, K. *dongnip jaju*) and domestic political reform, as promoted by Japan, suddenly hit a wall.

The Japanese Policy

What was Japan's position regarding Korea internationally at the time, and how did this view differ from previous perceptions and the perceptions it would come to hold in the future?

To address this question, let us begin with a series of four proposals submitted by Mutsu Munemitsu to the Japanese government's cabinet meeting on August 17, 1894:

Option 1. [Japan can continue to] regard Korea as an independent state, as we have done heretofore, entrusting all matters to its autonomous self-government, with which we shall not interfere and with which we shall allow no other to interfere, leaving it to decide its own fate.

Option 2. While officially acknowledging Korea as a nominally independent state, the Empire of Japan [can take an active role in] guaranteeing that independence by indirect or direct [means], either on a permanent or long-term basis, and prevent encroachments by other parties.

Option 3. As the British government previously recommended to the Japanese and Qing governments, [Japan can act to] guarantee

the safety of Korean territories in conjunction with the Qing.
Option 4. [Japan can] make Korea a neutral state by calling on the
Western states and Qing China to regard her in the same way as
Belgium and Switzerland are regarded in Europe. (*Kenkenroku*)

Here, Mutsu presents four potential choices for how Japan could
approach the Korea question. It is important to bear in mind that these
options were put forward by Mutsu immediately after the outbreak of
the First Sino-Japanese War and are thereby representative of the perspective Japan held at this particular time. All four proposals sought
to break the status quo in some way, albeit to varying degrees. Other
countries with differing interests would probably choose a different
policy for Korea from that of Japan, one that perhaps wasn't even
given articulation in any of Mutsu's four proposals.

The policy that Japan chose for Korea was the second option, which,
at its core, made Korea a de facto protectorate. This stance could also
be extrapolated from the way in which Inoue Kaoru referred to his
own Korea policy as being equivalent to "Britain's policy for Egypt."

The Japanese government's decision to take the second option also
signified that it had ultimately abandoned the third option of bilateral
joint protection and the fourth option of a multilaterally ensured neutrality.

As noted above, Mutsu's third proposal was considered upon the
conclusion of the Convention of Tientsin with the Qing in 1885, and
again during ceasefire negotiations after the outbreak of the First
Sino-Japanese War. As for the fourth option, as also noted above, this
was initially devised by Inoue Kaoru immediately after the Imo Incident in 1882, and, as an idea, more or less continued to occupy a
prominent position in the minds of the Japanese thereafter. This is evident from Prime Minister Yamagata Aritomo's *Gaikō seiryaku ron* (On
[Japan's] Foreign Policy, 1890), since it also proposed an identical plan
for achieving Korean neutrality. Incidentally, Yamagata's text is widely
known for promoting the ideas of a Japanese "sovereignty line" and

"interest line," and for its provision of a basic course of policy that would serve as the basis for Japanese imperialism.

While options 3 and 4 differed in form, they did have something in common: they were predicated on the eliciting of cooperation from other countries. This meant that by forfeiting these policies, Japan also forfeited collaboration with other countries in determining Korea's internati l position. The decision to do so was most likely a result of Japan judging that when hostilities between itself and the Qing had begun, it was competing interests over the Korean Peninsula that had led to the outbreak of conflict between them. Furthermore, Japan clearly realized that the ability to execute a policy that was free of foreign interference was wholly contingent on securing a victory in this war.

Japanese Retreat and Setback

In Article I of the Treaty of Shimonoseki, signed by Japan and the Qing on April 17, 1895, the Qing recognized Korea's "full and complete independence and autonomy." It is important to note that this differed in meaning from the first of Mutsu's proposals, which proposed that Japan acknowledge Korea's independence both in name and in substance. In addition to negating Korea's long-standing "tributary autonomy" vis-à-vis the Qing, over which the war had been waged, the article served as an indication that Korean independence would not be in the country's own hands, but rather that of Japan's. Indeed, the article indicated that Japan would thereafter be responsible for "guaranteeing the independence" of Korea.

The means that the Japanese used to carve out this position in Korea were the political reforms that had also served as the pretext for war with the Qing. The Japanese took exclusive control over reform of the country's domestic affairs, and in doing so, sought to render Korea "nominally independent." These were, of course, the Kabo Reforms implemented under the leadership of Inoue Kaoru.

As a corollary of this Japanese influence, then, the Kabo Reforms by no means perfectly aligned with Korean interests, and were affected by both the waxing and waning of Japanese power. Tensions between Japan and Korea continued to smolder, and these tensions would eventually come to the fore when Russia, France, and Germany made a diplomatic intervention into Japanese machinations after Japan had extracted the Treaty of Shimonoseki from the Qing.

Having defeated the Qing in the First Sino-Japanese War, Japan was ceded the Liaodong Peninsula under the terms of the Treaty of Shimonoseki. Only six days later, Russia, France, and Germany declared that Japanese possession of the Liaodong Peninsula made Korea "independent" in name but not in reality, calling it an obstacle to peace in the Far East and requesting that the Japanese government return it to the Qing. In the end, Japan had no choice but to yield to this triple intervention. A direct effect of this became immediately apparent in Korea.

Japanese prestige, on the strength of which the reforms had been forcefully implemented, was suddenly undermined. Those unhappy individuals who had been stripped of power as a result of the Kabo Reforms then gathered around Queen Min and plotted to recover their positions with Russian help.

Each and every Japanese measure was curbed by the Russian authorities, forcing them to a standstill. Moreover, a pro-Russian faction emerged within the Korean government that came to replace the one that had been cooperating with Japan. The separation of the court from the government was ultimately repealed, and many reforms began to be rolled back. At that point, Inoue Kaoru had no choice but to stand aside.

The Ŭlmi Incident and a Coup d'État

Imperial Japanese Army lieutenant general Miura Gorō took up the post of minister in Seoul on September 1, 1895, replacing the despondent Inoue Kaoru. It is clear that this personnel change was motivated by the predicament caused by the triple intervention of Russia, France, and Germany. However, it is unclear what solution the Japanese government was trying to bring about at the time. This is because one month later, Miura instigated an unimaginable act of barbarity.

From the night of October 7 to the early dawn of the following day, Japanese legation staff, garrison troops, and advisory officials broke in to Kyŏngbok Palace and attacked the sleeping quarters of Queen Min, murdering her and burning her corpse. This infamous assassination of Queen Min is also known as the Ŭlmi Incident. At the same time as this assassination, the perpetrators helped return the Taewŏn'gun to power and immediately sought to reorganize the Korean government. The emergent pro-Russia faction was purged, and the fourth Kim Hongjip Cabinet was formed, which once again advocated a pro-Japanese stance.

It may perhaps have been that Miura himself, tasked with resolving the situation, had carried out this coup d'état out of his own convictions. Nonetheless, it was inevitable that such a gross act of violence would be severely condemned. Had the criticism only been levied at Miura, then its influence may have been negligible. However, Japan, as a country, came under fire, and this had a tremendous effect on Japanese policy and national interests.

The fourth Kim Hongjip Cabinet continued to implement reforms, ordering a reorganization of the military and tax systems immediately upon its establishment. Moreover, they adopted the Gregorian calendar, officially rendering the 17th day of the 11th month of the ŭlmi year by the old lunar calendar as January 1, 1896. They also instituted the era name of Kŏnyang and promulgated the Short Hair Act (K. *tanballyŏng*). Nonetheless, a strong opposition to rejecting these traditional customs existed both within and without the government, with many resisting short haircuts as they considered it "a barbarian custom." In retrospect, these measures would prove to be a fatal misstep.

Throughout this period, the Kim Hongjip government was nothing more than a Japanese puppet regime. Kim Hongjip himself must have been well aware of this. Even so, he likely gambled on the potential offered by the reforms and dared to cooperate openly with Japan. He also took part in the efforts to cover up the truth of the assassination of Queen Min. But the sentiments that led him to do so would

Korean King Kojong (1852–1919) during his stay in the Russian Legation
Reproduced with permission from *Shashin de shiru Kankoku no dokuritsu undō* [The Korean Independence Movement in Photographs], pt. 1 (Tokyo: Kokusho Kankōkai, 1988).

never gain the understanding of others.

The movement to defend the neo-Confucian orthodoxy and to reject the heterodoxy of Western learning had long been inactive. However, this series of events gave it cause to once again come back to life, calling for people to "avenge the queen," and denouncing the promulgation of the Short Hair Act as a descent into "barbarity" that did away with Korea's status as "Little China." Eventually, the movement took up arms in January 1896 in an attempt to topple the government. This is known as the Early Righteous Army Movement.

As the movement spread across the country, troops were dispatched from Seoul in an attempt to suppress it. A dispatch of troops from Seoul, however, meant that the defenses left to protect the government in the capital were necessarily weakened.

Taking advantage of this vulnerability, the pro-Russia faction chased from power in the Ŭlmi Incident, including Yi Pŏmjin and Yi Wanyong, staged a coup d'état. With the assistance of sailors from the Russian navy who had entered Seoul, the faction brought King Kojong and his father out from Kyŏngbok Palace, moved them to the Russian legation in Chŏngdong District, and established a new government. This was on February 11, and the incident became known in Korean as the *Agwan p'ach'ŏn*, signifying the royal refuge in the Russian legation.

Fearing that the assassination of Queen Min would become an international incident, the Japanese Ministry of Foreign Affairs immediately recalled Miura and replaced him with Japanese statesman and diplomat Komura Jutarō. A decade later, Komura would become renowned for his diplomatic achievements in the Russo-Japanese War. However, he found himself without recourse to effective action when attempting to deal with the royal refuge in the Russian legation. This was the ultimate setback for Japan, which had relied on force to unilaterally advance into Korea following the outbreak of the First Sino-Japanese War and its victory therein. It did not simply signify the failure of its attempt at enacting Korean domestic political reform, which had been the casus belli for its war with the Qing. It also signified that Japan had no choice but to give

Komura Jutarō (1855–1911), Japanese statesman and diplomat
Photo courtesy of the National Diet Library, Japan

up on its goal of transforming Korea into a de facto protectorate, a goal that was supposed to have been achieved as an outcome of a Japanese victory in the war. Yet, as it transpired, in terms of achieving an upper hand in Korea, this Japanese victory had lost almost all value.

The Power Balance between Japan and Russia

That said, it would be far too simplistic to state that the replacement of a pro-Japanese regime with a pro-Russian regime would allow Russia to render Korea utterly submissive to it in place of Japan, which had long entertained ideas of a Korean protectorate.

Russia had naturally been concerned about Japan's rapid advance into Korea. Yet this did not necessarily translate into a policy of placing Korea in Russia's own sphere of influence. At the time of the outbreak of the First Sino-Japanese War, Russia continued to follow a policy of "maintaining the status quo" on the Korean Peninsula, as it had previously. However, the Japanese victory and Qing defeat came as a great surprise to Russia, and as such necessitated a revision of its Far East policy.

One aspect of this revision came with a shift in Russian interest from the Korean Peninsula to the Three Eastern Provinces of Qing China, also known as Manchuria. This shift became more pronounced when Russia gained interests in the form of railways and land concessions. Of course, this did not mean that Russia lost all interest in Korea, either.

Russia continued to push for the "maintenance of [Korean] independence," an interest that was also made palpably clear by its participation in the triple intervention against Japan. The confluence of this interest with that of the pro-Russian faction in Korea resulted in a successful expulsion of Japanese influence. Seen from this perspective, the situation that emerged as a result of the royal refuge in the Russian legation satisfied Russian interests, and meant that there was no need for Russia to make any further advances, especially militarily.

The Japanese were forced, albeit reluctantly, to accept this new state of affairs. Yet there was no way they would retreat from Korea entirely. The Komura-Weber Memorandum, exchanged in the Korean capital in May 1896, and the Yamagata-Lobanov Agreement, concluded in Moscow one month later, clearly demonstrated this resolve.

The former document stipulated that so far as the Korean government was concerned, the status quo would be maintained, and that both Japanese and Russian troops would be stationed in the country, while the latter established the specifics of Japanese and Russian interests in the country. In the words of Komura, it was "most appropriate" that Korea should be "jointly protected by Japan and Russia, for it provides [Korea] with the most benefit." In other words, Japan now saw the "joint protection" of Korea by itself and Russia as the optimum solution for the Peninsula.

Going back to the plans devised by Mutsu Munemitsu at the start of the First Sino-Japanese War, it was clear that by this point, all four of his proposals—including option 2—had now come to be entirely negated. However, if seen strictly from a Japanese standpoint, his third proposal of bilateral "joint protection" had been achieved, albeit through a replacement of the Qing with Russia. In many ways, this situation is reminiscent of that which had followed after the conclusion of the 1885 Convention of Tientsin, or indeed the situation that had existed up until the outbreak of Sino-Japanese hostilities in 1894.

There were, however, major differences between these situations. The Convention of Tientsin between Japan and the Qing had, after all, stipulated a withdrawal of troops, and there existed a diverse and multilateral range of guarantees for the "joint protection" of Korea by the Qing, who had yet to slip down the path of dynastic decline, and Britain and Russia, with which the dynasty had reached separate accords to varying degrees. By contrast, the "joint protection" of this later period was more unstable, as it was sustained by only two powers—namely, Japan and Russia—who remained at odds with one another.

In any event, the collapse of the Qing military as a result of the First Sino-Japanese War rapidly reduced the degree of direct military pressure that was being exerted on Korea from the continent. While this translated in relative terms to an expansion of Japanese influence on the Peninsula, the prompt appearance of Russia in the Qing's place helped to curtail Japanese expansion.

For Korea, the Russians and the Japanese were present both as friends and foes. Korea relied upon the two powers for protection, but also feared the threat of invasion that they simultaneously posed. However, at the same time, despite the general picture of Russian advantage and Japanese disadvantage, there was no longer any foreign power on the Korean Peninsula that occupied a position of *decisive* superiority. This signified that while Korea's international position subsisted in a state of legal ambiguity, there had, at least, been a return to a balance of power.

The Significance of the Royal Refuge in the Russian Legation

In the context of Korean domestic politics, the royal refuge in the Russian legation, as discussed above, constituted a coup d'état that succeeded in toppling the fourth Kim Hongjip Cabinet. The event was, historically speaking, highly significant, constituting much more than just a simple regime change and a shift in the direction of Korean foreign policy.

During these events, not only was Kim Hongjip, leader of the old regime, murdered, but Minister of Finance Ŏ Yunjung was killed while trying to flee, and Minister for Foreign Affairs Kim Yunsik was captured and banished. In this way, just as the Kapsin Coup had brought an end to the Independence Party and the radical reformists, the events surrounding the royal refuge were an eradication of the moderate reformist faction, both physically and politically. Following these events, the only ones left standing were King Kojong and the young pro-Russian officials, a situation that would paradoxically bring stability to the Korean government.

Kim Hongjip and the other so-called moderate reformists had frequently been involved in diplomatic negotiations since before the First Sino-Japanese War, and had been careful to maintain a distance from the Western powers. Indeed, the faction had focused its attention on Japan and the Qing, the two powers whose presence Korea felt most immediately, and had not invested its hopes and visions for the future in the distant West.

This had allowed Kim and the other moderates to become a party that acted as a balance among others inclined to arbitrarily side with one specific country, be it Japan, Qing China, or one of the Western powers. They ensured moderation by curbing extreme movements, and were careful to take into consideration Korea's traditional relationship with the Qing, albeit never allowing themselves to yield in the face of excessive Qing pressure. Their function and presence could be described as embodying the Korean "tributary autonomy" and the balance of power that it brought before the First Sino-Japanese War.

With the exit of the Qing, the moderates were forced to become "pro-Japanese," whether they liked it or not. Yet, precisely because of this commitment that they were forced to make, they faced eradication when Russia made its influence felt in the country. This historical process was exceedingly emblematic: it spoke of the end of a time in which the presence of the Qing or "tributary autonomy" had a direct impact on Korean politics.

Yet this was not the end of the story. If Korea's "tributary autonomy" had now come to an end, what form did the Korean state take in its wake? Many challenges still beset Korea and, while its "tributary autonomy" might well thereby have been relegated to the past, the Qing presence still loomed large in many of these remaining challenges.

3. The Rise of the Korean Empire

An Emperor Accedes to the Throne

On the 12th day of the 12th month of the *kabo* year in the traditional Korean calendar—or January 7, 1895, in the Gregorian calendar—King Kojong held a service at the Korean royal ancestral shrine in the presence of the royal family and all government officials. In the presence of the spirits of his ancestors, he recited an oath and proclaimed, "I shall break with the idea of relying on the Qing and establish a foundation of [Korean] autonomy and independence." A law was formulated based on this proclamation, containing the following passage:

> This country of Korea once proudly enjoyed autonomy and independence, yet at some point it became subject to Qing interference, such that its national prestige and power were gradually damaged.

It was soon decided that the king and queen of Korea should be given the same level of formal address as the emperor and empress of the Qing. Furthermore, Yŏngŭn Gate, which had been used to receive Qing envoys outside the walls of the Korean capital, was demolished. Both measures were meant to serve as a demonstration of a complete severing of *zongshu* relations that suggested Korean "reliance" upon the Qing.

Moreover, this took place when the Kabo Reforms were implemented under Japanese leadership. The proclamation made at the ancestral shrine had been another suggestion of Inoue Kaoru. Given that "the full and complete independence and autonomy" of Korea was stipulated in Article I of the Treaty of Shimonoseki some three months later, both the above wording and measures accorded entirely with Japanese plans. While the Koreans disliked the Japanese reforms that had been forced upon them, they did, however, at least agree with this project of rendering the country "autonomous and independent."

Given that Korea had previously exercised "tributary autonomy," and that it enjoyed "autonomy" in its domestic and diplomatic affairs as an axiomatic feature of this configuration, then Korea's pursuit of "independence" can be understood to be a process by which Korea was seeking to shed its "tributary" skin through the application of its pre-existing "autonomy."

For Korea, the merits reaped from entering into *zongshu* relations with the barbarian Qing and becoming a "tributary" of theirs were limited to two points. First, it meant that the Qing would not pose a threat to Korea. And second, it meant that the Qing would protect Korea from external enemies. A Qing polity that was devoid of all power could neither pose a threat nor protect, and gave Korea no reason to continue being its "tributary."

As such, the immediate issue for Korea after the value of its *zongshu* relationship with the Qing had been negated was the exchange of its "tributary" status for "independence," and its "tributary autonomy" for "independent autonomy." This aim endured through the Kabo Reforms, the Ŭlmi Incident, and the royal refuge in the Russian legation, and did not falter even when Korea was freed from the burden of Japanese pressure.

The royal refuge went in the opposite direction from that of the Kabo Reforms. It negated the Kabo Reforms' attempt at creating a modern political organization that separated the government from the court. Instead, the royal refuge restored the ability of the monarch to personally make all major political decisions (K. *man'gi ch'injae*), thus strengthening the monarchy considerably. This introduction of absolute monarchy was a response to the repeated coups d'état Korea had experienced, and can be understood as a natural consequence of the eradication of all the previously powerful officials and factions, such as the earlier Min regime. However, the fact that this absolute monarch was based in a foreign legation was an exceedingly bizarre circumstance that posed a threat to his dignity.

Although the Korean political situation had entered a period of calm after the royal refuge, this did not mean that the forces that opposed the government disappeared. One such opposition force was the Righteous Army Movement, which had already launched challenges to the government in various locations across the country. Since the movement itself was concerned only with the rejection of the project of Korean modernization, it mattered little whether the governing regime was pro-Japanese or pro-Russian. As such, the Korean government had to continue suppressing the movement even after the royal refuge. Japanese garrisons fought and repelled the movement in various places, and the movement was finally quelled in 1896.

Another opposing force was the Independence Club (K. *Tongnip hyŏphoe*) Movement. In late 1895, Sŏ Chaep'il returned to Korea from the United States at the invitation of the Kim Hongjip administration. He had previously participated in the Kapsin Coup with Kim Okkyun, fled to the United States, married an American woman, and become a U.S. citizen. Though not taking up any key position in the government, he did publish the first issue of *The Independent* (K. *Tongnip sinmun*) in April 1896, taking a firm stand for Korean autonomy and independence, and the country's opening up and enlightenment. Published thrice weekly, *The Independent* was the first newspaper to exclusively employ the native Korean Hangul script, and targeted not only intellectuals but the Korean masses as well. The Independence Club was founded in July of the same year by a group of men who sympathized with the views expressed by the newspaper.

These members of the Independence Club vocally criticized the government while also leading a movement that sought to make their arguments more tangible. A prime example was the construction of Tongnip Gate. The plan was to build an arched gate modeled after the

Left, Yŏngŭn Gate immediately prior to demolition; *right,* Tongnip Gate
Reproduced with permission from *Shashin de shiru Kankoku no dokuritsu undō* [The Korean Independence Movement in Photographs], pt. 1 (Tokyo: Kokusho Kankōkai, 1988).

Arc de Triomphe in Paris on the site of the demolished Yŏngŭn Gate that had been used when receiving Qing envoys in the past. The foundation stone was laid on November 21, 1896, and the gate was completed on November 20 of the following year, one year to the day. This movement gave eloquent articulation to how Korea's so-called "independence" first and foremost meant independence from the Qing, and the repudiation of Korea's traditional "tributary" status by the creation of a new "independent" Korea.

While the Korean government was troubled by the criticism leveled against it by the Independence Club, it had nothing against the club's calls for "independence," "loyalty to the monarch," and "patriotism." The government, too, was perfectly cognizant of the fact that King Kojong's inhabiting of the Russian legation was entirely unsuitable for such "independence."

While the king's return to the royal palace had already been debated on multiple occasions, it was concluded every time that it was too soon to make such a move. On February 20, 1897, one year into the royal refuge, King Kojong finally left the Russian legation and returned to the restored Kyŏngun Palace (present-day Tŏksu Palace). The new era name of Kwangmu was proclaimed in August, and he acceded to the throne as emperor on October 12. With this, the name of the country was also changed, to the "Korean Empire." After two years and ten months, the first step had at last been taken toward the establishment of the "autonomy and independence" that the newly dubbed Emperor Kojong had pledged before his ancestors.

In Pursuit of a Treaty with the Qing

That said, the perspectives and actions outlined above were Korea's and Korea's alone, and its unilateral choices had no bearing on how the Qing perceived its relationship with the country. Indeed, if the intention was to strip Korea of its "tributary" status and achieve "independence," the Koreans also had to reconfigure the terms of their relationship with the Qing. This is why I noted above that even after Korea's rejection of its "tributary autonomy," the Qing presence continued to pose a problem.

Once the Korean government had achieved a degree of domestic and international political stability, its representatives began approaching the Qing in this regard. On June 18, 1896, they contacted Tang Shaoyi (1862–1938), who was stationed in Seoul as trade representative to Korea, to discuss the possibility of concluding a treaty that would formally revise the Qing-Korean relationship.

Originally from Guangdong, and having studied in the United States, Tang had arrived in Korea together with Möllendorff. Throughout Yuan Shikai's tenure in Korea, Tang served as his aide and sometimes even in his place. When Yuan fled back to China on the eve of the First Sino-Japanese War, Tang continued mediating with Korea and Japan in Yuan's stead. Once Korea decided to rescind its previous arrangements with the Qing, such as the Regulations for Maritime and Overland Trade between Chinese and Korean Subjects, Tang's status in Korea was stripped of its legitimacy and he was forced to temporarily return to China. However, Tang was ordered back to Korea in the capacity of merchant representative in late 1895, as Chinese merchants who were based in Korea required protection.

In this role, Tang did not have the authority to conclude a treaty with Korea. However, as a result of his status and past experience in the country, he came to serve as the de facto representative of the Qing government.

During his time serving in this capacity, Tang was approached by a Korean interpreter named Pak Taeyŏng. Although Pak was, just like Tang, an individual of low status, the points of discussion that came up in their meeting were nonetheless important. Pak began this way:

> As [Korea] has rescinded its previous agreements [with the Qing], other countries might demand an explanation unless we conclude a new treaty.

In response, Tang offered Pak a curt refutation:

> How can a king housed at another country's legation be considered the ruler of an independent country? As matters stand, you neither possess the right of independence nor the capacity to dispatch envoys. All of this is stated in international law.

Pak persisted as follows:

> From what I hear, three thousand Russian soldiers are coming to Korea to protect Seoul. If this is true, our King may return to the palace. Might we not then dispatch an envoy?

Despite this effort, Pak was resolutely rejected by Tang:

> A country with another country's troops in its capital is naught but a protectorate of that other country. If you cannot be independent in the absence of those troops, your King remains without the right of independence. A country that must depend on another's protection for its existence is no different from a tributary state. Any dispatch of envoys or the like is unfeasible. Nor will international law

permit it. Even if your King were to dispatch an envoy to the Qing, it is unlikely he would be received with suitable ceremony. (*Qingji Zhong-Ri-Han guanxi shiliao* [Sources of Sino-Japanese-Korean Relations in the Late Qing Era])

The Korean argument was simple. Korea's "independence and autonomy" had already achieved international recognition with the Treaty of Shimonoseki. Hence, Korea needed to have it acknowledged by the Qing as well as by the rest of the world. And, as proof of this, Korea wanted to conclude a new treaty with the Qing, with whom Korea no longer had any formal diplomatic relations.

In response, Tang conveyed to Pak that it was difficult for the Qing to consider Korea to be an independent country, and impossible to treat it as such. This was because, with its king in a state of royal refuge, Korea was no different from a "protectorate" or "tributary," and it would be inappropriate to refer it as "independent."

The Qing Stance

This record of the meeting between Tang and Pak was drafted by the Qing, and I have yet to find any data on the subject originating from the Korean side. As such, there is naturally room for doubt as to whether these were the actual words exchanged by the two individuals. Yet at the very least, we can be fairly certain that this record accorded with the Qing perspective on the matter, which, if we were to summarize, was that it still wanted to look upon Korea as a "tributary."

This was not without precedent. When Vietnam, Burma, and the Qing's other "tributaries" became colonies of the great powers in the 1880s, the Qing was always trying to devise ways to show that these countries, even subjected to colonization, continued to constitute "tributaries" of the Qing. Examples included having other powers promise in their treaties with the Qing to not "injure its prestige" by negating the status of its tributaries, as well as ensuring that the ceremonial practices involved in tribute relations continued to be held.

Given that the Qing went to such lengths to find ways to continue to treat these colonized erstwhile tributary states as "tributaries," it was equally true that while Korea was no longer a "tributary," the Qing still wanted to consider it as such. However, the case of Korea was decisively different, in that Korea had not become a colony or a protectorate but was instead becoming "independent." For the Qing, this was without precedent.

It was for this reason that the Qing chose not to acknowledge Korea's "independent" status, and continued to shun its requests to sign a treaty and enter into a relationship premised on equality. What is interesting to note is how, when assuming such a stance, Tang Shaoyi always made these rebuttals in reference to the principles of international law.

This is highly significant, for it showed that a major change had taken place during the course of the First Sino-Japanese War. Whereas the Qing had previously campaigned for Korea's "tributary" status on the basis of the two countries' traditional *zongshu* relationship, Tang's actions signified that the legitimacy of this relationship was no longer tenable without recourse to a different normative paradigm: international law. Furthermore, this need to invoke international law to justify the Qing-Korean relationship was undoubtedly a consequence of the devastating loss of power and prestige the Qing had suffered as a result of its defeat in the war.

However, Tang also expressed his concern that if Korea gained the support of other countries in its quest to establish diplomatic relations with the Qing, and actually went ahead and dispatched an envoy who attempted to present his credentials to the emperor, it would be difficult for the dynasty to reject such a request in accordance with the principles of international law. Others also shared this argument and concern of his, including his home government.

The Qing government appointed Tang as consul general to Korea in late 1896. While on a day-to-day basis he was engaged in the consular protection of Chinese residents in Korea, his posting was itself also a preemptive measure. Indeed, by sending Tang as a diplomat of sorts to Korea, the Qing hoped he could work to prevent the Koreans from dispatching an envoy to China.

Since the Qing had to follow international law, Tang could not be given a title completely different from those of his diplomatic counterparts from other countries, as had been the case with Yuan Shikai prior to the outbreak of the First Sino-Japanese War. Rather than officially sending a diplomat to Korea in a ministerial capacity, the Qing instead decided to follow the precedents laid down by Britain and Germany and have Tang reside in the country as a consul general. The dispatch of a minister would suggest that the bilateral relationship was enacted on "equal" terms, and must therefore be avoided.

A Dead End in Negotiations

Tang Shaoyi entered Seoul as consul general on January 1, 1897. While the royal refuge had yet to come to an end, a new development was already underway.

King Kojong's departure from the Russian legation in February was naturally not something that could be decided upon arbitrarily and on a unilateral basis by the Koreans. The outcome was the result of ongoing negotiations with the Russians. After King Kojong acceded to the imperial throne and proclaimed the founding of the "Korean Empire," efforts to achieve Korean independence continued, which included the adoption of various measures that were intended to diminish Russian interests on the Peninsula. Examples of these included the discontinuation of the employment of Russian advisors and instructors, and the dismantling of the Russo-Korean Bank.

Such events were very much a response to that which the Independence Club had been calling for. Having succeeded in encouraging public opinion to favor Korean independence from the Qing, the group now engaged in an anti-Russia movement that resisted Russia's exceedingly pronounced advances. Such movements were no doubt underpinned by a desire to achieve independence for the country, not only in name but in substance as well. However, at the same time, these anti-Qing and anti-Russian sentiments were not wholly unrelated. It was also highly significant that the government accepted what the Independence Club had been calling for.

It is unclear how much of an impact the negotiations with the Qing, which were ongoing from the previous year, had on these developments in Korea. However, objectively speaking, it would appear to be the case that the negotiations had the result of doing away with Russian "protection," which had been so severely critiqued by the Qing, regardless of whether the Koreans were consciously engaged in such a policy.

The royal refuge and Russian "protection" of Korea had formed part of the basis for the Qing's rejection of Korean "independence" and its request to engage in treaty negotiations. However, the newly titled Emperor Kojong was now housed in Kyŏngun Palace, and the country had now done away with all vestiges of Russian "protection." It was from this new position that the Korean government once again attempted to open negotiations with the Qing.

Despite such efforts, however, the Qing attitude remained cold. Even when it came to the issue of King Kojong's ascension as emperor, Tang went so far as to initially state that since the Qing did not acknowledge Korea as an "independent and equal" country, they could neither "recognize the king as emperor" nor acknowledge Korea's attempt to take on an imperial title. Given such an attitude, concluding a treaty as equals was, of course, out of the question.

However, other countries did not make any conspicuous objections to the founding of the Korean Empire. Furthermore, as the Qing, too, had now come to assume an international position based on international law, it no longer could be said to occupy a position any more special than those of the other countries. As such, it became impossible for the Qing to subsist as the only country without treaty relations with Korea.

At the beginning of 1898, the Korean government once again

approached the Qing, and the other powers, one after the other, also began to suggest a recalibration of Qing-Korean relations. With this, the Qing, who had intended to put an end to the matter by appointing Tang Shaoyi as consul general to Korea, had no choice but to rethink their relationship with Korea.

Yet this did not mean that the stance of the Qing government changed overnight. Even if they were to forge a new relationship with Korea, the Qing were consistent in their desire "to demonstrate the age-old difference between master and servant," meaning an unequal and hierarchical relationship.

The scenario that the Qing therefore came to envisage was that the two countries should not dispatch an envoy to conclude a treaty, but rather a "trade agreement" instead. Indeed, the Qing continued to reject the format of parity proposed by the Koreans, in which an envoy would be sent to Beijing to conclude a treaty on an equal basis.

However, the Beijing-based Zongli Yamen was inundated with official recommendations from Russia, Japan, and Britain that argued to the contrary. In early July, the Qing therefore finally decided to receive a Korean envoy and engage in negotiations for the conclusion of a commercial treaty. Nonetheless, their plan was for the Korean envoy to serve not as a minister but as a chargé d'affaires, and for his diplomatic credentials not to be presented directly to the emperor but instead to be processed by the Zongli Yamen. Indeed, the Qing had no intention of compromising on their assertion that Korea was a lesser entity.

In Seoul, Tang responded to these developments by continuing to insist that an envoy be sent from the Qing side to Korea. He was adamant that doing things the way the Zongli Yamen wanted would make it difficult to demonstrate the traditional hierarchical relationship between the two countries, and that it would be a contravention of "international law" for a treaty envoy to not present his diplomatic credentials to the other country's head of state. Either way, this was a far cry from the format that was desired by Korea.

Signing a New Treaty between the Qing and Korea

It was the Qing Guangxu Emperor who brought an end, and a final decision, to these exchanges between Tang Shaoyi and the Zongli Yamen. On August 5, 1898, he instructed through imperial edict that all Korean requests should be met. While, in the end, this order was adapted into one which ordered the sending of a Qing envoy to Korea, it nevertheless provided a new opening in the Qing-Korean treaty negotiations that had made little headway since 1896, along with an actual date for execution. Shortly afterward, Xu Shoupeng, who had previously served in the United States, was appointed as minister to Korea. At the same time, Tang Shaoyi returned home to China to go into mourning for his father.

With Xu's appointment as Qing minister in Korea, personnel were completely replaced for the first time since the First Sino-Japanese War, and Qing-Korean relations finally advanced to a new stage. Xu arrived in Seoul at the start of the following year, presenting his diplomatic credentials to Emperor Kojong on February 1. On September 11, 1899, he concluded the Sino-Korean Commercial Treaty.

When we look back at this sequence of events, we may ask ourselves why it was that the Qing suddenly came to favor the conclusion of a treaty in the summer of 1898. To date, no historical sources have emerged which offer us an adequate answer to this question, so historians simply do not know. However, an examination of the international and domestic conditions in which such a decision was made is nevertheless perfectly possible.

Internationally, 1898 marked the start of the full-scale scramble for concessions in China. The leasing of Jiaozhou Bay to Germany and Lüshun (Port Arthur) and Dalian (Dalny) to Russia in March served to further intensify the great power rivalries in East Asia, and increased the risk of China's partitioning, known as *guafen* in Chinese, which literally means the "slicing up of a melon." Under such circumstances, the Qing moved toward the execution of the so-called Hundred Days' Reform of 1898.

The aim of the Hundred Days' Reform lay in reforming the Qing's long-standing bureaucratic apparatus along the lines of a modern state. It was based on a shift of worldview from the traditional Chinese vision of a world divided between "civility" and "barbarity" to one that emphasized an international vision of great power coexistence. It could be said that the Qing's dramatic change of course in August of that year to conclude a treaty with Korea was an emblematic reflection of this shift. Indeed, it was highly likely that this shift in worldview was heavily implicated in the Guangxu Emperor's decision to redefine Korea from its traditional "tributary" status to a "friendly state."

Thereafter, the Qing government did its utmost to ensure that all its "rituals of interaction" with Korea "conformed to the conventions of other countries" as much as possible. The following was also stated in the diplomatic letter of credentials carried by Xu Shoupeng:

> In recent years, we have begun to deem it just that all countries around the globe equally possess [the right to] autonomy and self-preservation. As such, China acknowledges the independent autonomy of Korea in accordance with Article I of the Sino-Japanese Treaty of Shimonoseki of Guangxu year 21 (1895).

While it states here that China will abide by Article I of the Treaty of Shimonoseki, in reality, the Qing only acknowledged Korean "autonomy" and never recognized its "independence," even after signing the Treaty of Shimonoseki. It was only some four years later that the Qing finally formally acknowledged that "autonomy" was inseparable from "independence," and therefore, that Korea was an independent state.

On August 17, 1899, some two weeks prior to the signing of the Sino-Korean Treaty of Commerce, the constitution of the Korean Empire, the *Taehan'guk kukche*, was promulgated. Article I declared, "The Korean Empire is an autonomous and independent empire recognized by all the countries of the world."

That Korea was able to make this proclamation was another consequence of its success in concluding a treaty, and thereby a relationship of parity, with the Qing. Four and a half years after that oath to the royal ancestors, the day had finally come when Korean independence was achieved.

4. The Year 1900

The Structure of "Independent Autonomy"

If we take the preceding discussion to be correct, then Korea's independent autonomy can be said to have been brought about by a delicate combination of international factors.

The movement that sought Korean independence with guidance from the Japanese after the First Sino-Japanese War was soon frustrated by opposition from the Korean government and Russia. Of course, even if Korea had achieved independence, the fact that Japan's goal was to turn Korea into a protectorate casts doubt on whether Korea would have been truly independent. Even if Korea had genuinely become independent, it is likely that it would not have stayed that way for long. From the Korean perspective, the country would probably have gained nominal independence without substantive autonomy.

King Kojong's decision to take refuge in the Russian legation in Seoul in 1896 decisively put an end to the Japanese-led reforms and movements toward independence. Yet at the same time, the king's move also overturned the overwhelming position of superiority that Japan enjoyed in Korea and brought about a delicate balance of power that pitted Japan against Russia. Korea came to renew its quest for independence amid this new situation and, in doing so, turned to the Qing for help.

Yet despite Korean calls for help, the Qing stance had changed little. The Qing, who had now come to embrace "international law" as the criterion for the resolution of such matters, argued that Korea's "protection" by the Russian legation prevented it from being able to recognize the Korean government's independence, and was therefore reluctant to conclude a treaty with the country.

The situation changed when Russia obtained a lease on Lüshun and Dalian in late March 1898. This move, which constituted a new stage in the partitioning of China, served to raise momentum for Qing reforms and also to change the Qing stance on its foreign relations. At this point, the Qing finally came to recognize its erstwhile Korean tributary as a friendly state. The Qing retroactively approved the ascension of Kojong as Korea's emperor and, furthermore, the establishment of the Korean Empire. And, in 1899, the Qing concluded a trade agreement with the country on terms of equality.

What we must take note of here is that the Russian lease on Lüshun and Dalian, despite putting the Qing as well as Korea and Japan on their guard, did not initially impart any significant fluctuations in the arrangement of forces that maintained the delicate balance that had existed since 1896. The balance of power that was produced by Japan withdrawing politically from the Korean Peninsula and by Russia not launching any decisive military action in Manchuria remained intact.

In April 1898, immediately before the Russian lease of Lüshun and Dalian was finalized, an agreement was concluded between the Japanese foreign minister, Nishi Tokujirō, and the Russian minister to Japan, Roman R. Rosen. The pact confirmed and expanded on the Yamagata-Lobanov Agreement, calling for Korean independence and nonintervention in Korean affairs, and also establishing Japanese economic predominance in Korea. Through its signing of the agreement, Japan gave tacit consent to the Russian lease on Lüshun and Dalian.

Prior to this agreement, Japan proposed a Manchuria-Korea exchange, stating that as "Manchuria and its coastal regions fall entirely outside the scope of Japan's interests and relations," Japan was desirous of exchanging it for the right of "Japan to take complete control of the duties involved in advising and assisting" Korea. But no agreement was ever reached on this proposal. The fact that an agreement was never reached, or indeed the fact that one did not even need to be reached, was an indication that the existing balance of power in Korea remained in play.

This balance of power was a re-creation of the military vacuum that had existed on the Korean Peninsula prior to the First Sino-Japanese War, and which had guaranteed Korean "tributary autonomy." While it is true that Korea lost its nominal "independence" with the withdrawal of Japan, the balance of power still allowed it to recover substantive "autonomy."

In order to convert its traditional status of "tributary autonomy" into that of "independent autonomy," it thus became necessary for Korea to maintain the balance of power that had sustained its "autonomy," and also to reject its status as a Qing tributary. It was able to do just that in the intervening years between the founding of the Korean Empire in 1897 and the signing of the Sino-Korean Treaty of Commerce in 1899.

To briefly recapitulate: In order for Chosŏn Korea and the later Korean Empire to subsist as an "autonomous" entity, it was essential that two conditions be met. First, that the international balance of power maintain a military vacuum on the Korean Peninsula. And second, that Korean "independence" be recognized by other countries, including Qing China.

While Korean "tributary autonomy" was, prior to the outbreak of the First Sino-Japanese War, successfully sustained by the first condition, Korea struggled with the second condition, as different countries possessed different perspectives on the issue of its independence. However, at the same time, this clash in perspectives conversely helped contribute to securing Korean autonomy. When the Kabo Reforms began in 1894, Korea enjoyed independence but was denied substantive autonomy. The opposite was true during King Kojong's refuge in the Russian legation. It was not until 1899 that both conditions were at last fulfilled.

The Russian Occupation of Manchuria

Securing "autonomy" was, therefore, the prerequisite for Korea's independent autonomy. And, this "autonomy" could only be lastingly secured so long as the international balance of power endured. However, as early as 1900, this prerequisite began to crumble. This was due to the outbreak of the Boxer Rebellion and the ensuing Russian occupation of Manchuria.

The Qing had lost their traditional influence over the Korean Peninsula following their defeat in the First Sino-Japanese War and the annihilation of their Beiyang army. Even so, they could not remain indifferent to Russia or Korea, given that they bordered both countries. Although the Qing might no longer field a particularly large externally facing military force, so long as they held Manchuria, they continued to function as a deterrent which kept Russia away from the Korean Peninsula. In this manner, the Qing likewise contributed to the power balance which emerged in the postbellum period of the First Sino-Japanese War.

However, if a powerful military force were to appear in Manchuria, the situation would radically change. And it did: when Russia occupied the region.

Russia had possessed significant interests in Manchuria for some time, including the Chinese Eastern Railway and its lease on Lüshun and Dalian. However, a military occupation achieved through the deployment of a large army was an endeavor of an entirely different scale from that of the simple maintenance of regional interests. Russia subsequently demanded unbridled control of Manchuria and started putting pressure on the Qing to this effect.

During this expansion of influence, Russia also began to set its sights on the Korean Peninsula as well. While this did not translate into any immediate action, it slowly began to develop an interest in the adjacent Korean Peninsula during its management of Manchuria. The form of interest that Russia came to harbor toward the Peninsula was analogous to what the Qing once did: an interest that had required

Korea to assume a subordinate position to the Qing for the purposes of safeguarding the security of the Three Eastern Provinces that constituted Manchuria.

King Kojong's decision to take refuge in the Russian legation frustrated Japan's Korea policy, and Japan ceased to take a proactive political stance on the Korean Peninsula after the signing of the Komura-Weber Memorandum and the Yamagata-Lobanov Agreement. This is partly because the Japanese were happy with the existing power balance. The signing of the Nishi-Rosen Agreement was a symbolic demonstration of Japan's satisfaction in this regard.

In accordance with the Nishi-Rosen Agreement, Japan limited the scope of its negotiations with Russia to the Korean Peninsula and refrained from discussing Manchuria. This was a stance made possible by the weak military threat posed by forces in the regions north of the Peninsula. Yet all of this changed when Russia occupied Manchuria and the balance of power became unstable.

Since the Meiji Restoration, Japan had assumed that if the Korean Peninsula fell into enemy hands, especially Russian hands, Korea would become a serious threat to the Japanese archipelago, like "a blade hanging over one's head." After 1900, Japan was accordingly forced to strengthen its political and military interests on the Korean Peninsula. Moreover, this time it had to do so in connection with Manchuria, which had hitherto been treated as a separate issue.

Caught between the two, the Korean government was unable to handle the situation with its existing policy stance. From the outset, Korea did not possess the military power to resist its neighbors. Furthermore, the balance of power that was vital for securing its "autonomy" had instead been maintained by the great powers, and Korea simply made use of the position that equilibrium created for it. However, now that the interests of these great powers—Russia and Japan—had changed, that approach no longer sufficed. It then became necessary for Korea to play an *active* role in maintaining the balance of power.

Korean Neutrality

The year 1900 was a turning point that ushered in a period of frenetic diplomatic negotiations among Korea, Russia, and Japan about the international status of the Korean Peninsula. Particularly noteworthy during this period was the proposal for Korean neutrality and the reactions the proposal provoked.

The proposal for Korean neutrality was first broached to Japan in August 1900 by Cho Byŏngsik, the Korean minister to Japan. It was subsequently brought up on successive occasions by both Korea and Russia in a variety of forms, up until the outbreak of the Russo-Japanese War in 1904.

The aims of the Korean government in making such a proposal were to maintain the country's independent autonomy, as well as to maintain the necessary balance of power on which that independent autonomy was wholly contingent. Until this point, this balance of power had only been maintained in a de facto fashion and was by no means stable. Korea wanted to make the balance of power a more permanent feature of regional security by replacing it with a multilateral arrangement that was enacted on legal terms.

The aims of Russia were naturally not wholly consistent with those of Korea. Russia's proposal for Korean neutrality was drafted and supported by Finance Minister Sergei Witte. Korean neutrality was an inseparable part of Russia's plan for managing Manchuria. The Russians wanted to preempt a Japanese invasion of the Korean Peninsula before the Chinese Eastern Railway had been completed and before Manchuria was fully under Russian economic and political control.

However, from the Japanese perspective, the proposal to make Korea "a country whose neutrality [was] guaranteed by other states" was, as a proposal, in no way coterminous with an attempt to internationally ensure the preservation of the status quo on the Korean Peninsula. This was because the power balance was already crumbling as a result of Russia's occupation of Manchuria.

At the end of August, Konoe Atsumaro, president of Japan's House of Peers and of the East Asia Common Culture Society, met with Cho Byŏngsik and duly explained the situation:

> A neutral country must at least possess the means to defend itself and it must be located among several countries whose interests are immediately affected by the existence of that country. Thus, the countries pledge that if one of them were to harbor designs on the neutral country, the other countries shall unite to punish that country. Korea cannot be said to satisfy these criteria, as only Russia and Japan have interests there. While others may have interests in the form of railways and mines, it matters little to them whether Korea stands or falls. As such, while they are not likely to object to Korean neutrality, there is also no reason for them to go as far as taking up arms if the Russians were to pursue their ambitions as they please following the establishment of Korean neutrality. In such a situation, they will simply retreat and take a passive position. It will only be Japan who will have to oppose the Russians, even at the cost of war. The Russians cannot bring their ambitions to the fore so rashly, and will bide their time until their management of Manchuria is complete, and they stand a chance of defeating Japan in war. Even if Japan knew of Russia's ambitions, an agreement on neutrality would mean that we would have no choice but to silently wait for Russian preparations to be completed. (*Konoe Atsumaro nikki* [Diary of Konoe Atsumaro], 1968–1969)

Japan had, in the first place, abandoned the concept of Korean neutrality by, at the very latest, the outbreak of the First Sino-Japanese War. This was because it was only the Qing and Japan that, at the time of the war, had "interests in Korea." After the war, however, Russia came to take the place of the Qing and, alongside Japan, began to take an interest in Korea as well. This resulted in a situation that was analogous to that which existed when the First Sino-Japanese War had broken out, except that the Qing had been replaced by Russia.

Japan found it difficult to believe that any form of multilaterally guaranteed neutrality for Korea would be effective if it was just Japan and Russia that had an active interest in Korea. Moreover, compared with the time when the Komura-Weber Memorandum had been issued, which had effectively acknowledged a de facto "joint protection" of Korea, the contemporary state of military power relations was a world apart. Seen from the perspective of the plans that Mutsu Munemitsu had devised at the start of the First Sino-Japanese War, it already appeared as if the circumstances no longer allowed for the enactment of his fourth recommendation of Korean neutrality, nor for his third recommendation of joint protection.

In this way, from 1900 onward, the Korean and Japanese positions started to diverge decisively. Korea, in pushing for its own neutrality, aimed at somehow maintaining both the balance of power and its own independent autonomy in the face of the military threat Russia posed from Manchuria. And, at the same time, this Korean quest for neutrality was an attempt to resist Japanese and Russian attempts at managing the Korean Peninsula in conjunction with Manchuria. By making the Korean Peninsula neutral under multilateral guarantees, Korea would be kept apart from the situation in Manchuria for the time being, thereby contributing to its self-preservation.

In contrast, Japan could no longer look upon the issue of Manchuria as separate from that of the Korean Peninsula. Faced with the Russian occupation of Manchuria and the disintegration of the balance of power, Japan was no longer able to entertain the idea of simply dividing up its interests on the Peninsula and in Manchuria with Russia, nor was it able to refrain from interfering in Manchuria, as had been the case at the time of the Nishi-Rosen Agreement. The various distributions of power in Manchuria and on the Korean Peninsula had become intimately intertwined, and Japan had come to see the two regions not separately, but as a unified and indivisible issue. This is the reason that proposals such as the Manchuria-Korea exchange, the delimitation of spheres of influence on the Peninsula, and the creation of a Korean protectorate were brought up in negotiations, and the reason that Japan saw these proposals as life or death matters.

Seen from this standpoint, any Korean neutrality that obstructed a Japanese advance would doubtlessly work in Russia's favor. For Japan, this was the reason that proposals for Korean neutrality appeared from the outset as nothing but a form of collusion between Korea and Russia. Eventually, Japan would have to choose between either avoiding or waging a war with Russia. However, regardless of the choice it made, the two options were alike, in that they both would eventually sacrifice the independent autonomy of Korea.

The Anglo-Japanese Alliance and the Russo-Japanese War

The first Anglo-Japanese Alliance was signed in London on January 30, 1902. This alliance recognized Japan's "special interests" in Korea and obviously had the aim of countering Russia's southward expansion in the Far East. If we examine the intentions of both parties, however, then the history that unfolded around the time also comes into relief.

It is well known that ever since Russia's occupation of Manchuria, the Japanese government had one camp that favored reaching an agreement with Russia, with statesman and prime minister Itō Hirobumi at its core, and another group of leaders who favored an alliance with Britain, including Yamagata Aritomo and statesman and politician Katō Takaaki. The issue was whether to first approach Russia or Britain about reaching an agreement on Japan's interests and establishing a collaboration. Moreover, the selection of an ally was directly linked with the question of how to deal with Korea.

To secure Manchuria, Russia sought to build a barrier against military threats from the south. Korean neutrality was one aspect of this strategy. If Japan were to choose to ally itself with Russia and do nothing else, then regardless of the extent to which Japan was permitted to advance into Korea, it was probable that Japan would only be able to do so partially and would never extend to the entire peninsula.

By contrast, if Japan were to prioritize an alliance with Britain, such limitations and restrictions on Japan's Korea policy would disappear.

In the first place, since the mid-1880s, Britain had argued for Korean subordination to the Qing as a means to prevent Russia from launching a southward expansion. It was even said that Britain's support for the Qing at the time constituted a de facto alliance with Japan. When the Qing were defeated in the First Sino-Japanese War and became an unreliable ally, British support was offered to Japan instead. As such, the idea of Korean subordination to Japan was already a given.

Japan chose alliance with Britain. This choice was a consequence both of Japanese foreign minister Komura Jutarō's preference for an active expansion into Korea and of the pro-Japanese stance that Britain had pursued after the conclusion of the First Sino-Japanese War.

The decision naturally did not mean an immediate end to Russo-Japanese cooperation or that military confrontation was inevitable. Through their signing of a treaty of alliance, Japan and Britain put pressure on Russia. Eventually, Russia agreed to withdraw its troops from Manchuria. The agreement Russia reached with the Qing on April 8, 1902, to return Manchuria to Qing control was significant in that it led to this withdrawal of soldiers on Russia's part. The Russians agreed to pull out all of their troops in three stages, spaced six months apart.

Yet, just as Komura had suspected, Russia did not carry out its second withdrawal. Instead, it remained in Manchuria and showed signs of recommencing its southward expansion. In the end, attempts to reconcile Japanese and Russian interests on the Korean Peninsula broke down, and the Russo-Japanese relationship ultimately collapsed. This rupture determined the fate of Korea.

Conclusion

On February 10, 1904, the Russo-Japanese War broke out.

On February 23, 1904, the Japan-Korea Treaty of 1904 was signed.

The latter recognized the seizure of strategic locations in Korea by the Imperial Japanese Army. The Russo-Japanese War was fought in Manchuria, which was Qing territory. In order for Japan to send troops to Manchuria, it had to secure all of the Korean Peninsula.

At this point, the Korean Peninsula's international position was to be decided bilaterally between Japan and Korea. And it was the power dynamic between the two that would ultimately determine that fate. This dynamic also more or less dictated the fate of Korean autonomy. As a result of Japan's victory in the Russo-Japanese War, that fate became irreversible.

On October 16, 1905, the Treaty of Portsmouth was announced.

On November 17, 1905, the Japan-Korea Treaty of 1905 was signed.

The latter made Korea a Japanese protectorate. Korea thereby lost its autonomy in both name and substance. Eventually, Korean resistance to this situation intensified. However, Japanese suppression of that resistance consequently became greater as well. The antagonism between Japan and Korea became more severe. This was the starting point on a road that led to Japan's eventual annexation of Korea.

Korean independent autonomy thus lasted between five and ten years at most. Moreover, autonomy over a unified Korean Peninsula has not been achieved since then. This is a solemn fact of history.

It would appear that this historical reality also constitutes the origins for the advocation of Jucheism and the current declaration of autonomous diplomacy on the part of Korea.

This book started out with a discussion of the East Asian situation in the sixteenth century, when the world was becoming more unified as a result of global flows of silver. That moment constituted the historical starting line of the Korean Peninsula's geopolitical importance. Inseparable from that was the sudden rise to prominence of the Japanese archipelago, the Liaodong region, and Manchuria.

The question was how to sustain each polity while also adjusting and stabilizing the power relations between them. From the seventeenth century onward, this became a historical challenge on which hinged the order and peace of not just the Korean Peninsula but of all East Asia.

One answer was the parallel existence of Japanese-Korean neighborly relations and Qing-Korean *zongshu* relations during the Edo period, and another was the "tributary autonomy" of the second half of the nineteenth century. In all of this, the role played by the Qing was extremely crucial. A general survey of history shows that as long as the Qing remained stable, Korean autonomy was assured to some extent.

This is clear if we once again hearken to the words of the young George Curzon on the eve of the First Sino-Japanese War:

Her [Korea's] intrinsic weakness is in reality her sole strength; for were she powerful enough to render her own alliance an appreciable weight in the scale, she might be tempted to adopt a course of action that must infallibly result in final absorption. The foolish persons who, from interested motives, prate to her of independence are inviting her to sign her death warrant. Alone she has no more strength than a child in arms; though, so long as her three great neighbours continued to regard each other from a watchful distance, Korea, which lies between, might escape the armaments of each. Now, however, that the gage of battle has been thrown down between two of the three, her territorial integrity, to which the three are virtually pledged, is vanishing into thin air, and will be difficult to

re-establish. An international guarantee has sometimes been suggested as a stop-gap; but Russia, we may be sure, would decline to step beyond her existing pledge, which she probably already regrets, while China could hardly be asked to guarantee her own vassal. My conviction is that the only hope of continued national existence for Korea lies in the maintenance of her connection with China . . .
(*Problems of the Far East: Japan, Korea, China*)

This is very much an argument based on contemporaneous British interests, and the vocabulary and tone sound conspicuously imperialistic to modern ears. That he both praises the significance of *zongshu* relations with the Qing and is negative toward Korean "independence" can be taken as signs of this. However, when it comes to what Curzon has to say about "tributary autonomy" and the balance of power it brought, he is on point and even prophetic.

He was right to state that "now . . . that the gage of battle has been thrown down between two of the three," as happened with the Sino-Japanese and Russo-Japanese wars, "Korea's territorial integrity" and the "continued national existence for Korea" would "vanish . . . into thin air." This sequence of events acted to negate the presence of the Qing.

The primary causes of this Qing negation were the First Sino-Japanese War and the Russian occupation of Manchuria. When the Qing became weaker and the "great neighbours" could no longer "regard each other from a watchful distance," Korean "independence" became nothing but an "illusion . . . from which [would] spring future disturbances," a prediction made by Curzon elsewhere. As such, the cool-headed British diplomacy that had supported the Qing in its initially stronger position switched to favor Japan and to conclude the Anglo-Japanese Alliance.

One person who must have been most well acquainted with the "illusory" nature of "independence" for Korea was Kim Hongjip. This is why he supported the Qing's Korea policy and assisted with the Japanese Kabo Reforms. By chance, he followed the same pattern as Britain's

Far East policy. This was undoubtedly because he possessed both a dispassionate situational awareness and a firm set of convictions.

While the British approach did not cause any serious trouble, both of Kim Hongjip's efforts were unsuccessful. In the end, he resigned himself to the fact that his ambitions would never materialize and lowered the curtain on his own life. His story is a tragedy, if ever there was one.

The question was how to adjust and stabilize the power relations surrounding the Korean Peninsula. This historical challenge resulted in a great loss of life, ranging from nameless commoners and soldiers to a prime minister and a queen. Even so, it remained crucial, not only until the Russo-Japanese War at the start of the twentieth century but also for East Asian international politics today. Even as states rise and fall and the conditions of military power change with the passage of time, it would appear that the principles that underpin this challenge remain the same.

The crisis on the Korean Peninsula continues even today. Although we bear witness to it and are aware that it is an extremely pressing issue, we find ourselves unable to offer an effective response.

This is why the history discussed in this volume is likely not a tale of times long past. While historical events cannot be repeated, they can be used as references when searching through the various options and possibilities presented by the past as we devise a guide for the future. I believe that the Japanese people of today can also find issues here that we need to contemplate seriously.

Principal References

If I were to simply list all the sources consulted when writing this book, not only would it be very bothersome to compose, it would also be so long and meaninglessly dry that it would bore you, the reader, as well. I will content myself with citing some of the main works, with a focus on Japanese texts that are not given as much attention these days as they have been given in the past, along with a short commentary on each.

In writing this book, the following four academic texts were the ones that I referred to time and again.

Tabohashi Kiyoshi. *Kindai Nis-Sen kankei no kenkyū* [Research on Early Modern Japanese-Korean Relations], parts 1 and 2. Tokyo: Hara Shobō, 1973. First published in 1940 by Chōsen Sōtokufu Chūsūin (Tokyo).

While the title employs an old Japanese term for "Japanese-Korean relations" that is no longer in use, the book's contents would be better termed a magnum opus on the history of international politics in the Far East from the nineteenth century to the outbreak of the First Sino-Japanese War. The scope is vast, the descriptions detailed, and it is a timeless masterpiece that remains fresh and deserves to be read again and again. The Chinese text from primary sources does not indicate Japanese readings, so it requires Chinese reading proficiency. I wish there were an index.

Nakamura Hidetaka. *Nis-Sen kankeishi no kenkyū* [Research on the History of Japanese-Korean Relations], parts 1–3. Tokyo: Yoshikawa Kōbunkan, 1965–69.

This is another classic. It is an absolute must if you want to know the details of East Asian foreign relations from the Muromachi period (1336–1573) to the establishment of the Edo *bakufu* in 1603. Again, don't be fooled by the outdated language used for the term for "Japanese-Korean relations" in the title. Deft use of the index enables the reader to access a treasure trove of historical sources and facts. However, since the book itself is a collection of academic research papers, there is no coherent story, making it a bit difficult to read. You might also be puzzled by how to read some of the primary sources as well.

Tashiro Kazui. *Kinsei Nit-Chō tsūkō bōekishi no kenkyū* [Research on the History of Early Modern Japanese-Korean Relations and Trade]. Tokyo: Sōbunsha, 1981.

This is a monumental work that looks at Japanese-Korean relations in the period between those covered by Tabohashi and Nakamura, with a focus on Tsushima's trade and economy. The detailed accounts and extensive statistics provided by the book are truly astonishing, a result of the author's tireless collection and analysis of historical sources. While the detailed nature of the sources themselves was no doubt one reason why the author was able to compile such a text, from the perspective of someone who works on Chinese economic history, I am truly envious of the author's ability to work at such a high standard.

Moriyama Shigenori. *Kindai Nik-Kan kankeishi kenkyū: Chōsen shokuminchi-ka to kokusai kankei* [Research on the History of Modern Japan-Korea Relations: The Colonization of Korea and International Relations]. Tokyo: University of Tokyo Press, 1987.

This is a meticulous inquiry into relations between Japan and Korea from the First Sino-Japanese War to the annexation of Korea. It is significant in that it analyzes the internal structural dynamics of the Korean government as inseparable from the actions of other countries. However, the excessive density of the arguments makes it far from an easy read. I would have liked a few more pages dedicated to citations of primary sources and an introduction of evidence to support the claims made, but all in all, this book is indispensable if you want to know about how the colonization of Korea took place in the context of international relations.

In addition to these works, there are some academic papers that I must mention, although they might be a bit too technical.

Iwai Shigeki, "Henkyō shakai to 'shōgyō būmu'" [Chinese Frontier Society and the 'Commercial Boom'], included in Iwai Shigeki, *Chōkō, kaikin, goshi: Kinsei Higashi Ajia no bōeki to chitsujo* [Tribute, the Maritime Prohibition, and Private Trade: Trade and Order in Early Modern East Asia] (Nagoya: University of Nagoya Press, 2020, originally published in 1996), is a wonderful work that depicts the lively commercial boom that took place along the Great Wall and in the Liaodong area in the late Ming and early Qing periods.

For information about relations with Russia, which many Japanese readers might struggle to understand, the following are excellent and are used in many university syllabi: Sasaki Yō, "The International Environment at the Time of the Sino-Japanese War (1894–1895): Anglo-Russian Far Eastern Policy and the Beginning of the Sino-Japanese War," *Memoirs of the Research Department of the Toyo Bunko*, 42 (1984), esp. pp. 5-25; and Sasaki Yō, "1880-nendai ni okeru Ro-Chō kankei: 1885-nen no 'Daiichiji Ro-Chō mitsuyaku jiken' o chūshin toshite" [Russo-Korean Relations in the 1880s: Centering on the "First Russo-Korean Secret Agreement Incident" of 1885], *Kan* (Journal of Korea), 106 (1987); and Sŏk Hwajŏng, "Rosia no Kankoku chūritsu-ka seisaku: Witte no tai-Manshū seisaku tono kanren de" [Russia's Policy for Korean Neutrality: In Relation to Sergei Witte's Manchuria Policy], *Suravu kenkyū* [Slavic Studies], 46 (1999). For information about Japanese diplomacy on the eve of the Russo-Japanese War, a stimulating read is Chiba Isao, "Takakuteki dōmei, kyōshōmō no mosaku to zasetsu" [Groping For and Failing to Achieve Multilateral Alliances and Networks], in *Kyū gaikō no keisei: Nihon gaikō 1900–1919* [The Formation of Old Diplomacy: Japanese Diplomacy, 1900–1919] (Tokyo: Keisō Shobō, 2008).

While there are many survey texts and books written for general audiences on the periods of Chinese and Korean history for the period covered in this book, there are not very many good ones, especially among recent publications. It might be because of the authors' lack of ability or it might be because political interests and considerations are prioritized, but the result is that the historical sources are used arbitrarily and unreliably.

However, if I were to name a few books that are worth referencing, there is Kishimoto Mio and Miyajima Hiroshi, *Sekai no rekishi 12: Min-Shin to Ritchō no jidai* [World History 12: The Time of the Ming, Qing, and Chosŏn Dynasties] (Tokyo: Chūōkōron Shinsha, paperback ed., 2008; originally published in 1998), a first-class work on the general histories of the Ming, Qing, and Chosŏn dynasties. Kishimoto Mio, *Higashi Ajia no "kinsei"* [East Asian "Early Modernity"] (Tokyo: Yamakawa Shuppansha, 1998), should be considered a rendering of the world history background for the aforementioned paper by Iwai that discusses the Ming frontier, so it is a good idea to read the two together. Examples of works that discuss Japan, Tsushima, and Korea around the same period are Tashiro Kazui, *Kakikaerareta kokusho: Tokugawa, Chōsen gaikō no butaiura* [The Rewritten State Letters: Behind the Scenes of Tokugawa-Chosŏn Diplomacy] (Tokyo: Chūōkōronsha, 1983); and Tashiro Kazui, *Wakan: Sakoku jidai no Nihonjin machi* [The Japan House: A Japanese Settlement in the Period of National Isolation] (Tokyo: Bungeishunjū, 2002). These are continuations of the work by Tashiro that I mentioned earlier, but she has widened the context to diplomacy and exchange in a detailed yet clear manner. For modern Korean history, I keep close at hand Kasuya Ken'ichi, *Chōsen no kindai* [Korean Modernity] (Tokyo: Yamakawa Shuppansha, 1996). It is written more like a textbook, but it is exceedingly convenient as it unerringly contains all the basic historical facts.

Lastly, I would like to mention three of my own works:

Okamoto Takashi. *Zokkoku to jishu no aida: Kindai Shin-Kan kankei to Higashi Ajia no meiun* [Between Dependency and Sovereignty: Modern Qing-Korean Relations and the Destiny of East Asia]. Nagoya: University of Nagoya Press, 2004.

Okamoto Takashi. *Ba Kenchū no Chūgoku kindai* [Chinese Modernity as Seen from the Perspective of Ma Jianzhong]. Kyoto: Kyoto University Press, 2007.

Okamoto Takashi. *Chūgoku no tanjō: Higashi Ajia no kindai gaikō to kokka keisei* [The Birth of China: International Relations and the Formation of a Nation in Modern East Asia]. Nagoya: University of Nagoya Press, 2017.

The first focuses on Qing-Korean relations in the 1880s and the involvement of Japan, Britain, the United States, and Russia. The second is a critical biography of Ma Jianzhong, who also appears in this book, and includes an annotated translation. It is particularly detailed about the time around the Imo Incident. The third addresses, from a historical perspective, the rise of the modern Chinese nation in the context of international politics, in which Japanese-Qing-Korean relations and their changes in the 1880–90s exerted a vital influence. I recommend these to readers who want to know more about the historical sources and events that I was unable to discuss in detail in this book.

Index

223

Hong Taiji *42, 46–47, 48, 49, 50–51, 52, 57*
Hongwu emperor (China) *35*
Huang Zunxian *15, 85, 86, 87*
Hulun Yehe tribe *40*
Hundred Days' Reform *201–2*
Hunehe tribe *37*
Hŭngsŏn Taewŏn'gun. *See* Taewŏn'gun

About the Author

Okamoto Takashi is professor in the Department of Historical Studies, Faculty of Letters, at Kyoto Prefectural University. Born in 1965, he graduated from Kobe University and obtained his Ph.D. in literature from Kyoto University. Okamoto served as associate professor at the University of Miyazaki before assuming his current position, where he specializes in East Asian and modern Asian history. He has published many books on modern Asian and Chinese history, of which three have won awards: *Kindai Chūgoku to kaikan* [China and the Maritime Customs System in Modern Times] (Nagoya: University of Nagoya Press, 1999), recipient of the Ohira Masayoshi Memorial Prize (Ohira Masayoshi Foundation), focuses on the structure of the modern Chinese state derived from Qing China's customs system; *Zokkoku to jishu no aida: Kindai Shin-Kan kankei to Higashi Ajia no meiun* [Between Dependency and Sovereignty: Modern Qing-Korean Relations and the Destiny of East Asia] (Nagoya: University of Nagoya Press, 2004), which won the Suntory Prize for Social Sciences and Humanities (Suntory Foundation), examines Qing-Korean relations since the nineteenth century; and *Chūgoku no tanjō: Higashi Ajia no kindai gaikō to kokka keisei* [The Birth of China: International Relations and the Formation of a Nation in Modern East Asia] (Nagoya: University of Nagoya Press, 2017), recipient of the Kashiyama Junzo Prize (Kashiyama Scholarship Foundation) and the Asia-Pacific Prize (Asian Affairs Research Council), details the evolution of the foundations of modern China. Other English translations of his works include *Asia Reoriented: A New Conception of World History* (Tokyo: JPIC, 2022), a translation of *Sekaishi josetsu: Ajia shi kara ichibō suru* (Tokyo: Chikuma Shobō, 2018), which reconsiders world history from an Asian historical perspective.

本書に掲載されている写真画像の著作権の確認および許諾については万全を期しております が、長い年月を経て所有者が不明となっているものも一部ありました。 お気づきの点がございましたら、下記までご連絡ください。

　　　　　　　　　　　　　　一般財団法人　出版文化産業振興財団（JPIC）

（英文版）世界のなかの日清韓関係史：交隣と属国、自主と独立
Contested Perceptions: Interactions and Relations between China, Korea, and Japan since the Seventeenth Century

2022年3月27日　第1刷発行

著　者　　　岡本隆司
英　訳　　　公益財団法人日本国際問題研究所
発行所　　　一般財団法人出版文化産業振興財団
　　　　　　〒101-0051 東京都千代田区神田神保町2-2-30
　　　　　　電話　03-5211-7283
　　　　　　ホームページ　https://www.jpic.or.jp/

印刷・製本所　　大日本印刷株式会社